RUG WEAVING TECHNIQUES

RUG WEAVING

B.T. BATSFORD LTD | London

PETER COLLINGWOOD

TECHNIQUES

BEYOND THE BASICS

photography by David Cripps

First published in Great Britain in 1990 by
B.T. Batsford Ltd
4 Fitzhardinge Street
London W1H 0AH

Designed by Ray Carpenter

ISBN 0 7134 6733 9

Designed and produced by
Bellew Publishing Company Ltd
7 Southampton Place, London WC1A 2DR

Printed in The Netherlands by Royal Smeets Offset.

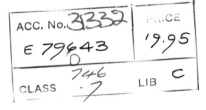

Contents

Introduction

IF THERE IS one thing of which I am completely sure it is that my designing ability is slight. I have only to hear a few bars of Bach or to glance at a Paul Klee to have it hammered home that any creativity I have is of a different, infinitely lower, order. This is not a new or depressing realization. Having missed the art school experience, I was never misled into thinking of myself or my work as in any way inspired or of great importance.

I regard myself as a weaver making workman-like textiles as well as I know how, from average quality materials, and in designs which aim at an unpretentious simplicity, which do not shout, 'Me, me . . . look at me'.

Though I missed art school, I did have two years excellent training in several production workshops in England. It was Ethel Mairet, for whom I worked for three rather stormy months, who later wrote to me with an important piece of advice, 'Make your workshop as critical as mine and you may get somewhere'. This concept of criticizing hand weaving, both my own and others', and rejecting what was unadventurous and purely traditional or used inappropriate materials or structures, made a deep impression on me. Implicit in it was the idea that a cloth simply because it bore a 'Woven by Hand' label was not automatically superior to a similar machine-woven cloth. To be justified, hand weaving had to produce what power looms could not or would not.

These ideas, linked to a quite irrational desire to live from shuttle-throwing, shaped the way I had to think and work. If I was to succeed – and those people telling me that abandoning medicine was foolish made some sort of success all the more imperative – I had to produce at a low cost and, therefore, at a fast rate. As my chosen field was rugs, this implied jettisoning all the traditional methods of rug weaving, such as knotting, tapestry, weft wrapping, because though they gave the greatest design possibilities, they were all extremely slow. This coupling of design potential with slow production has been a constant fly in my ointment, but I think shaft-switching has at last uncoupled them.

It was this desire for quick production – I aimed at three rugs per week – i.e. for the ability to make rugs by simple selvage-to-selvage shuttle-throwing, not by intricate hand manipulations of weft, that led me to explore shaft-controlled rug techniques. With such methods the weaver is taking advantage of the complexity of his or her loom; threadings, tie-ups, different treadlings and weft sequences all contribute and can be permutated endlessly. Many of the methods I used were developed from those used in cloth weaving; so they were weft-face versions of weaves in which normally both warp and weft are visible. This proved a rich vein, especially when at last, like many other weavers before me, I invented Summer and Winter and so entered the realm of block weaves. The three-end block weave, a structure I now use almost exclusively, came later; it was quickly noted down while I tied my shoe-lace on a rug in this technique, spotted in a London furniture store.

These modest conversions and near-discoveries make me think of the Industrial Revolution. In textiles, it enabled machines to do with greater speed and precision what human hands had already been doing for millenia. The inventions brought about a change in the amount of yardage woven in a day, not a change in its type or quality. Such speed-increasing inventions continue today with water and air jet looms. But I believe strongly that there are discoveries still waiting to be made of quite another type, unconnected with picks per minute. As examples of this type, already in existence, I would include Mr Miyajima's beautifully simple loom which gives triaxial interlacing and perhaps my own shaft-switching system. Both offer the hand weaver possibilities denied him before, not in the realm of speed, but in structure and personal control over design.

This exploration of techniques took concrete form in *The Techniques of Rug Weaving* which I wrote to avoid further teaching. Since its publication nearly twenty-two years ago, I have taught continuously. That large book arguably has enough in it to keep most rug weavers busy for life, so is there any need for more information on the subject as contained in this book? But just because all those facts exist in print does not stop my mind – or the minds of other weavers – from continuing to think of new methods. Such discoveries may be thought merely academic exercises, intellectual games; though to an out-and-out structuralist such as myself, they are engrossing games. But their real importance lies in the way they point the weaver along a certain path when designing.

This is because every technique has its own specific range of design possibilities; it allows the weaver to make this type of motif, not that; it can be used with two colours, not three; it produces a rug that is the same or different on its two sides; and so on. By playing with a technique, discovering these rules, finding out what it can do easily, what it wants to do, and maybe how it can be cajoled into doing something which at first seems impossible – it is in this way that the weaver learns the special language of a technique and can use it economically and to its best advantage when designing a rug.

This approach implies that every technical or structural innovation has, implicit in it, design possibilities waiting for the weaver to unearth and utilize. But a simple equation stating more techniques equals more good rug designs is, of course, fallacious, because there is another important ingredient in designing and that is the ability to make the correct decision when two or three equally valid options present themselves.

I think one can only acquire that ability by looking, by educating one's eyes with a constant stream of good images. (How do I define correct and good? I cannot.) Written words about proportion, contrasting textures, colour theory, types of symmetry may all be perfectly true but they will not help the weaver at that moment of decision. At that crucial moment, whether working on paper or at the loom, the weaver can only appeal to the ultimate referees, his or her eyes, and rely entirely on their judgement. I believe the appeal is more likely to bring the right answer if the referees have constantly played over things of beauty in the weaver's environment; unconsciously absorbing ideas of colour, proportion and texture, an absorption which is purely physical and wordless. The reader will find that I have not dealt with the design of each technique described but I hope the colour plates of samples, specially woven to accompany the text, will say something in this regard.

The loom on which the rug techniques and designs are to be worked is of great importance. American weavers who are surprised when they see my looms and the size of their timbers would be overwhelmed by Scandinavian rug looms. There, looms up to 13 feet (4 metres) wide are made and used. The warp sticks are thicker than the main timbers in many small floor looms, warp beams have ratchets at both ends to avoid any torsion, cloth beams are turned with elaborately geared handles – everything is on a gigantic scale. But should such a monster loom be the longed-for ideal, the twinkle in every rug weaver's eye? I think not, as its only advantages are that a large rug can be woven in one piece or that several rugs can be woven side-by-side at the same time.

Early on, lack of money and space forced me to work on a much smaller, though strong, loom, a secondhand four-poster countermarch loom by the great English maker, George Maxwell. I soon realized its weaving width of 44 inches (1.1 metres) was no great disadvantage, because if I joined accurately woven strips, I could weave a rug of any width. The widest object I have woven on it was a corduroy rug 26 feet (8 metres) wide, made in strips a comfortable 2 feet (60 cm) wide.

So I usually advise weavers to use a loom with, say, 4–5 feet (1.2–1.5 metres) weaving width. This is ideal for the usual floor rug, 3–4 feet (0.9–1.2 metres) wide; the extra width in the loom is because of the difficulty of weaving at a loom's full weaving width. This, coupled with a good method of joining strips, means the weaver can tackle a rug of any width and, moreover, do it by himself.

The problem with a loom of this size is that it may need strengthening if it is to be used exclusively and often for rugs; and here we touch on the subject of altering a loom, about which I have strong feelings.

Consider a loom used by a working weaver, perhaps in a poor country. It is a shaming and ramshackle collection of bars and sticks, with not a carpenter's joint or a decent bolt in sight. But it works. The weaver knows what is essential – even warp tension, good shedding, easy-running shuttles, a straight beat – and if it has these features, he pays no attention to the ill-assorted branches and lashings which hold it all together.

I have much sympathy with this very practical attitude and have never looked with awe on my, always secondhand, looms. If I consider that screwing a piece on here or sawing a bit off there will strengthen or improve it – or more importantly make it do something new and atypical -- then I do this with no feeling of desecration. This attitude is probably influenced by my first loom, made after a visit to a London craft shop. It was botched together from two old deck chairs and resembled two inkle looms, face to face. I then added four shafts, then pedals, then a beater with a laboriously-made reed – and it still had neither warp nor cloth beam. So, from the start, the concept of a loom as a device susceptible to alteration and improvement was deeply ingrained in me.

Quite different, and understandably so, is the attitude of a weaver buying a brand new loom. It arrives perfectly packed and with exhaustive assembly instructions, sometimes even with tools for assembly. It then stands in the living room in all its hand-rubbed glory, giving off oily smells from each perfectly finished surface. It is an object for admiration, almost veneration, so its possessor would be extremely reluctant to interfere with it in any way. This is the concept of textile equipment as art object.

But whatever concept of a loom the weaver has, he or she must realize a rug is an extreme textile and so demands an extreme loom for its making. Ideally, the loom should have great strength, good depth, excellent tension control and a heavy beater.

The strength is needed so that the high warp tension, necessary for good weft-face weaving, can be provided and maintained. How high that tension should be can be understood when one sees the hefty chains and turn-buckles fixed to the two warp bars of a horizontal ground loom used for durrie-weaving in India. That the weaver's children are allowed to bounce on such a warp, like a trampoline, shows his faith both in the warp material and its unalterable tension.

As well as general strength, the depth of the loom is very important. Imagine two pairs of warp threads, one pair twice the length of the other, and all four threads stretched at the same high tension. Now try to open a shed in each pair, i.e. pull one thread up, one down. It is obvious that this will prove easier with the longer pair; the greater length of yarn – even if it is practically inelastic like linen – having more give in it. In other words, with a highly tensioned rug warp, shedding is easier the deeper the loom happens to be.

The horizontal warp-extender I use on one of my looms gives it a depth of 12 feet (3.6 metres) at the start of a rug, though it obviously decreases during weaving. The vertical extender also effectively increases the depth of the loom.

Good control of warp tension implies the use of a large ratchet on the cloth beam with two or more pawls, or alternatively some form of gearing, like a worm drive.

When considering the beating in of the weft, again refer back to a simple horizontal ground loom. With such a loom, it is done bit by bit across the width of the rug with a heavy wood or metal hand beater, all the weaver's strength driving home just a short section of the weft at a time. It is obviously hard to duplicate that kind of compression with a single swing of the over- or under-slung batten of a frame loom. But it is surprising what effect extra weight can have. The force with which the batten strikes depends partly on the weaver's strength of arm but largely on its momentum. Its momentum is its weight times its speed; so doubling its weight means it strikes twice as hard even though swung at the same speed. Over the years, my battens have become heavier and heavier; each addition at first seeming a burden but soon feeling normal and anything lighter feeling just plain flimsy.

For easy shedding with a taut warp, the shafts must rise and fall, rather than just rise; this means a countermarch action. The often-expressed dread of making the lam-to-pedal ties on such a loom derives from the experience of doing so on a really small loom. If a loom is of a decent size, the weaver can sit inside and tie up in relative comfort. I sit on a padded board above the pedals and do not regard this as a specially onerous task. Many loom-makers have devised tie-up systems, using chains, slotted braid, standard length cord loops, all in an attempt to featherbed the weaver in this job. But none of these systems has the *infinite* adjustability of the traditional snitch knot. Good loom cord lasts a long time; I am only gradually replacing the cords which have hung from lams for over twenty-five years.

Obviously the above advice is for an ideal rug loom and such is only necessary for a serious weaver of many rugs. A lighter, smaller, loom will produce a rug or two, but the loom may suffer in the process and the weaving will be more difficult and slow.

Many of the ideas in this book originated in classes I have given, mainly in America. Sometimes they were stimulated by a student's unexpected question, sometimes they were born out of desperation to find something new to satisfy the fastest student's needs. Sometimes, and more rewardingly, they came from the student's own application of the 'What happens if . . .' attitude I try to instil. To the latter I offer thanks and regret that I have recorded only the names of Vincent Carleton, Penny Druitt, Linda Eschels, Eisha Katar-MacGregor, Jean Young and Diana Ziegner.

As my teaching has concentrated on flat rugs made in plain weave, twill and block weaves, it is these techniques which figure most prominently in this book. Also I have not come across anything new in other fields, such as knotting, and weft wrapping. The reader will find the three-end block weave is very fully described, especially the application to it of shaft-switching, as that is the only method I now use in my own rug production.

I cannot avoid hearing references to *The Techniques of Rug Weaving* as the weaver's bible. But I hope what follows, together with the original work of many weavers worldwide, shows that a fundamentalist attitude to it is flawed; it is certainly not the last and only word on the subject of rug weaving. Though this book is really an addendum to, an update on, that bible, I have tried to make it reasonably self-sufficient.

To avoid needless repetition, occasional references are made to *The Techniques of Rug Weaving*. They appear in the form (TRW p. 34), meaning see page 34 of that book.

Peter Collingwood, May 1990
Old School, Nayland,
Colchester, UK.

Weft-face Rugs in Plain Weave

Warpway or Pick-and-pick Stripes

Producing cross-stripes of two colours, each consisting of some even number of picks, is perhaps the simplest weft-face rug technique and presents few, if any, problems. If, however, the two wefts are strictly alternated in the so-called pick-and-pick sequence, the result is narrow stripes or lines of the two colours running in the warp direction. Using a warp with four working ends per inch, there will be four of these lines per inch, each lying over a warp thread. This commonly-used technique leads inevitably to problems at both selvages where the outermost warp thread is missed by both wefts. Disregarding methods in which the two wefts are either linked outside the selvage (making it untidy), or float over or under two ends (making it loose), there are at least three distinct ways, described below, of solving this very basic problem. (It is assumed that there is an odd number of working ends in the warp.)

Grierson Method

(TRW p. 104 onwards. First described by Ronald Grierson in *Woven Rugs*, Dryad Press, 1952)
When moving from a solid colour to these stripes, there are always two options. Either the previously-used colour or the new colour becomes the edge stripe; see *Fig. 1(a)* and *(b)*, respectively.

A different method of work is needed for each of these possibilities. See Plate 1 at top.

(a) So that the previously-used colour, A, becomes the edge stripe

Stop weaving A when it is passing *over* the selvage end. This could be at the right or left side, depending on the direction A was thrown in the first shed. Here it is at the right; see *Fig. 2(a)*.

Start B, the new colour, at the same side and throw to the left; see *Fig. 2(a)*.

Now wrap A downwards between ends 1 and 2, tying down the starting float of B, and then throw it in the next shed; see *Fig. 2(b)*. This is the only place where B reaches the selvage.

The weaving then proceeds normally for this method, with B always missing the selvage and A always wrapping twice downwards to compensate for this before being thrown; see *Fig. 2(c)*.

(b) So that the new colour, B, becomes the edge stripe

Stop weaving A when it is passing *under* the selvage end. Start B at the opposite side; see *Fig. 2(d)*. The two colours are now emerging at the left selvage exactly as in *Fig. 2(b)*, but with the colours reversed.

Weave normally; A is now the colour missing the selvage and B has to wrap twice downwards before being thrown.

Notes
— *The result of this method is a perfect upper surface, but with the forward 'jumps', where A or B misses the selvage, clearly visible as spots on the back. See Plate 1 (pp. 14–15), top section, back view.*
— *If the weft is wrapped upwards, instead of downwards, it forms a float under two ends at the selvage.*
— *Disobeying the above rules results in the rug being woven upside-down, with a perfect underside.*

Counter-changing colours

To counter-change the colours, so that the stripes shift sideways over one warp end, as in *Fig. 3(a)*, two picks of one of the wefts must be woven in succession. It does not matter which weft is used, but if the one forming the outermost stripe is chosen there are no problems at the selvage; see the two picks of dark weft, A, at lower arrow in *Fig. 3(b)*, and the change of the colours above.

If the colour *not* forming the outer stripe weaves the two picks (see the two picks of B, now *not* forming the outer stripe, at upper arrow in diagram), then the selvage has to be handled as shown at the right. One weft, B, passes over two ends making a float, which is immediately bound down by weft A diving down between ends 1 and 2 before it is thrown. Plate 1 (pp 14–15), top section, shows this counter-changing.

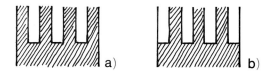

Fig.1

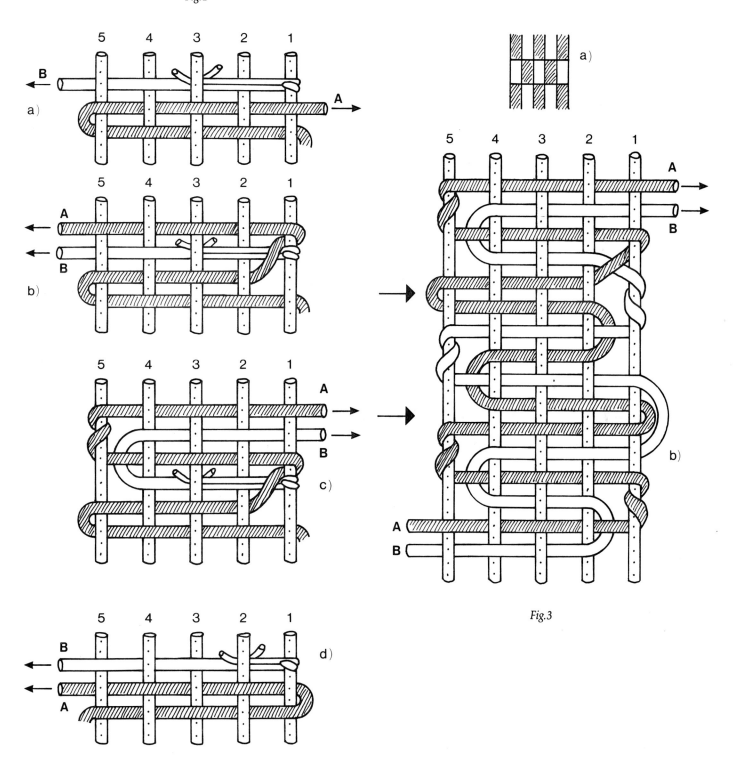

Fig.2

Fig.3

FRONT

Plate 1 (see pp. 12, 16–18)

BACK

Navaho Method 1

Though the two wefts are linked in this method, the link is pulled inwards, avoiding any lumpiness at the selvage.

(a) So that the previously-used colour, A, becomes the edge stripe

Stop weaving A when it is passing *over* the selvage end.

Start new colour, B, at the opposite side and place it over A; see *Fig. 4(a)*.

Throw A in the next shed, leaving a loop at selvage; see small arrow in *Fig. 4(b)*.

Throw B, pulling this loop around to the back, as in *Fig. 4(c)*. This pick misses the selvage.

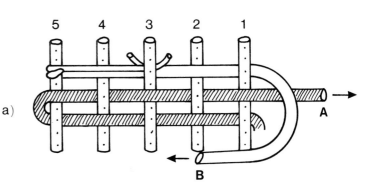

Fig.4

(b) So that the new colour, B, becomes the edge stripe

Fig.5

See Plate 1 (pp. 14–15), central section.

Stop weaving A when it is passing *under* the selvage end; at left in *Fig. 5(a)*.

Start B at the opposite side and pass it under A as it emerges from the shed; see *Fig. 5(a)*.

Throw A, ensuring it crosses over B, and tighten it so that a loop of B is pulled to the back, as in *Fig. 5(b)*. A misses the selvage.

Throw B normally; see *Fig. 5(c)*.

Notes
— The result is a perfect upper surface, but on the back the two outer ends are covered with the same colour.
— This is a very simple method as no wrapping or unusual working is required at the selvages.
— To counter-change the colours, weave two consecutive picks of B, either one more in Fig. 4(c) *or in* Fig. 5(c).

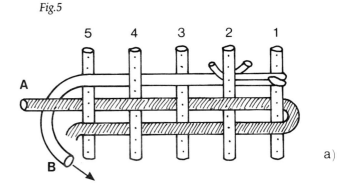

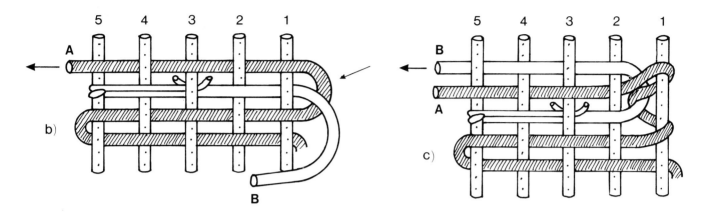

b)

c)

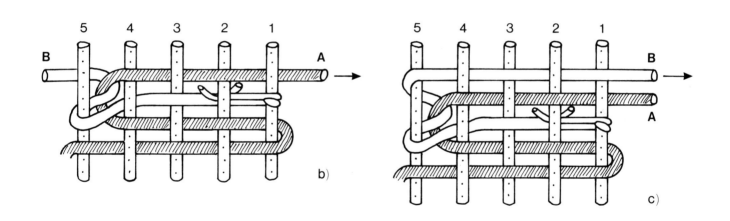

b)

c)

Navaho Method 2
(Seen on blanket from Coal Mine Mesa,
Tuba City, Arizona.)

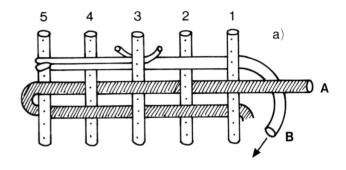

Fig. 6

There is no one-colour stripe over the selvage end with this method. So it is the stripe *next* to the selvage which is referred to in the headings below.

**(a) So that the new colour, B,
becomes the stripe next to the selvage (as in** *Fig. 6[a]*)

Stop weaving A when it is passing over the selvage end.

Start B from the opposite side, making it lie under A when it emerges from the shed; see *Fig. 7(a)*.

Enter A into the next shed, but pass it under the selvage end, 1 (which is lowered), so it is floating under two ends, 1 and 2; see *Fig. 7(b)*.

Bring B *upwards* between these two ends, thus tying down the above float, and then throw it in the next shed; see *Fig. 7(c)*. B should be pulled tight enough to make this crossing point lie in the centre of the thickness of the rug. See Plate 1 (pp. 14–15), bottom section.

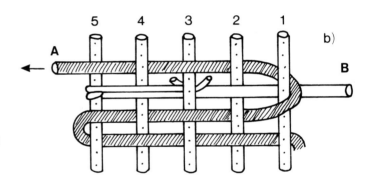

**(b) So that the previously-used colour, A,
becomes the stripe next to the selvage (as in** *Fig. 6[b]*)

Stop weaving A when it is passing under the selvage end.

Start B at the opposite side and bring it over A as it emerges from the shed; see *Fig. 8(a)*.

Enter A into the next shed, but pass it over the raised selvage end 5, so it is floating over two ends, 4 and 5; see *Fig. 8(b)*.

Take B *downwards* between these two ends, thus tying down the above float, and then throw it in the next shed; see *Fig. 8(c)*.

Notes
— *The result of this method is that both colours wrap alternately around the selvage, giving a pleasant fine striping.*
— *There is no back or front in this completely reversible and excellent method.*
— *It is really a very clever, but extreme, use of Crossed Wefts in Contrary Motion, the outer areas of cross-stripes being reduced to the absolute minimum.*
— *The simplest way to counter-change colours is to weave two picks of the weft which arrives second at either selvage; i.e. in* **Fig.** *7(c) weave another pick of B to the right, or in* **Fig.** *8(c) weave another pick of B to the left. Plate 1 (pp. 14–15) bottom section, shows these two counter-changes.*

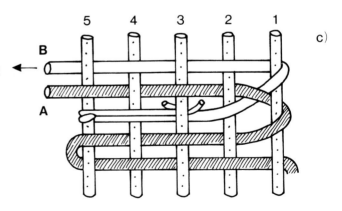

Fig. 7

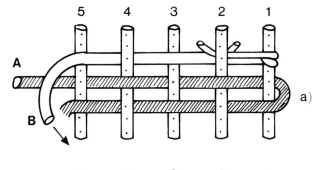

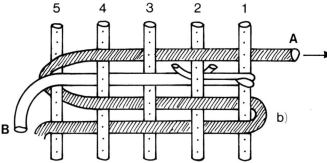

a)

b)

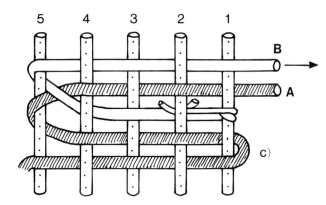

c)

Fig.8

Overcast Selvage

This ingenious way of producing an overcast edge is really a special application of the Gauze Soumak technique (TRW p. 190), confining it to the two outer working ends on both sides of a weft-face rug.

Throw the weft from left to right normally, as at bottom of *Fig. 9*.
Change the shed.
Twist the outer selvage end, 1, over the next end, 2.
Insert the shuttle through the opening thus formed and then into the shed. Make it leave the shed through a similar twist in the last two ends, 7 over 6; see *Fig. 9*.
Beating causes the warp ends to untwist and the weft then lies as in *Fig. 10*, which includes the next pick.

As seen in Rajasthan, the outer two working ends are three to four times thicker than the rest of the warp. The loom is a horizontal ground loom, the sheds being produced with a shed rod and leashes. The thickened outer two ends go over and under the shed rod in the usual way, but the outermost one is not attached to a leash (see top of *Fig. 9*) as it would normally be. The initial shed, as described above, is given by the shed rod and goes right across as required; the second shed, with the rod pushed away and the leashes raised, leaves the two outer ends level with each other and therefore easy to manipulate in this way.

A rising shed loom with a floating selvage at each side will give almost the same conditions.

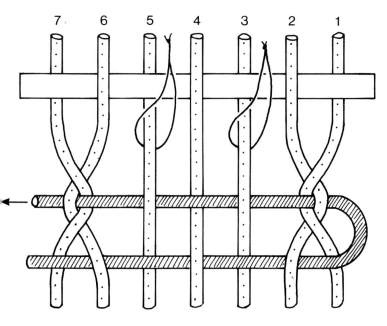

Fig.9

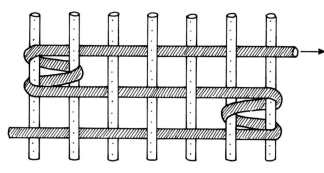

Fig.10

Crossed Wefts

In the Crossed Weft technique, two wefts starting either from opposite selvages in the same shed (i.e. in Contrary Motion; see *Fig. 11*, bottom) or from the same selvage in successive sheds (i.e. in Parallel Motion; see *Fig. 11*, top) actually cross each other one or more times as shown. In both types of motion, the crossing has a very characteristic structure. The first weft to move at a crossing inevitably floats over two ends, but this is tied down by the other weft which floats under the same two ends. So in *Fig. 11*, bottom, the dark weft passes over ends 5 and 6 and is tied down by the light weft passing under the same two ends. Failure to work this correctly produces a weakness at the crossing point.

This simple crossing manoeuvre which reverses the relative position of the two wefts usually produces horizontal and vertical stripes in areas, the shapes of which are freely controllable; see Plate 2 (p. 22). Some further possibilities are now described.

Areas of Spots

These can be produced in at least two ways.

(a) Parallel motion

As *Fig. 12* shows, one method is worked with Crossed Wefts in Parallel Motion, the two wefts having one crossing pick followed by four straight picks. The alternating areas show interrupted pick-and-pick stripes. There is not a great deal of contrast between the two areas; see Plate 3 (p. 22).

(b) Contrary motion

The second method, worked in Contrary Motion, has a third weft the same colour as the background of the spotted area; see *Fig. 13*. The unspotted areas have stripes of unequal width. It is interesting that when the areas are counter-changed, only two wefts are needed, as shown in *Fig. 14*. Plate 4 (p. 23) shows this technique.

Increasing the Width of Cross-stripes

Cross-stripes of two picks are usually narrower than the vertical pick-and-pick stripes, and can cause a design using both types of stripes to look unbalanced. *Fig. 15* shows a way of increasing their width to three picks. It needs four wefts, two of each colour; two of these always move in Parallel Motion, crossing twice, the other two weave single picks straight across in sequence.

If woven as in the diagram, the 3/3 cross-stripes will be in the central area with pick-and-pick stripes on either side.

Note
— It is the straight, non-crossing picks that determine which areas show which type of striping. So by simply reversing their sequence, (i.e. by starting with a solid line weft, not a dotted one, for the third pick up in **Fig. 15***), the areas can be easily counter-changed; see Plate 5 (p. 23), which also shows the difficulty of producing neat selvages.*

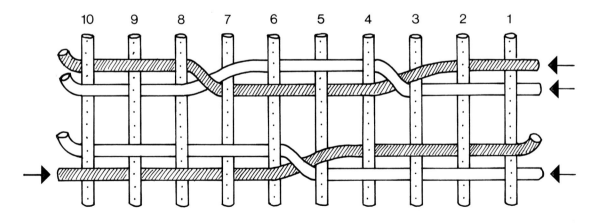

Fig.11

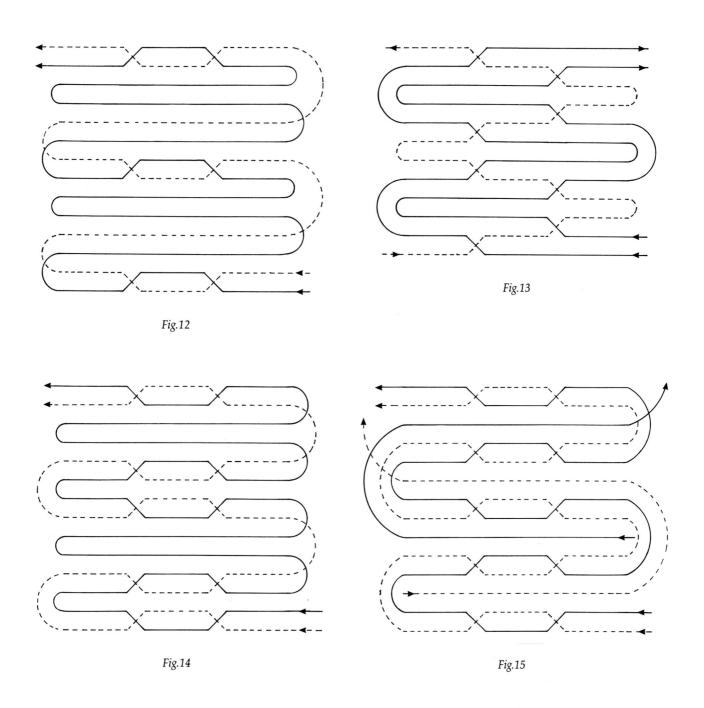

Fig.12

Fig.13

Fig.14

Fig.15

Plate 2 (see p. 20)

   Plate 3 (see p. 20)

Plate 4 (see p. 20)

Plate 5 (see p. 20)

Combining with Meet and Separate Weave

Combining Crossed Wefts with the principle of Meet and Separate Weave (i.e. a weft never reaches the opposite selvage but always returns to its own) leads to an interesting result, shown in *Fig. 16*.

Starting with wefts A and B at opposite selvages, bring them into the centre and then out of the shed.

Change the shed and cross them in the normal way, but take them out of the shed short of the selvage: A between raised ends 10 and 12, and B between 2 and 4.

Change the shed, take A to the right, bringing it out of the shed between raised ends 3 and 5, that is one end less far than B.

Change the shed and take A to the right selvage, noticing that it floats over two warp ends, 3 and 4.

Weave two more picks with A on ends 1 to 3.

Now bring B to the left selvage; as it enters the shed it ties down the float of A. Weave two picks with B on ends 12 to 14.

This is the complete cycle; two are shown in *Fig. 16*. Four picks have been woven in every area and the wefts are back at their starting positions. Repeating this cycle exactly leads to four definite areas: solid colour A at the right and solid colour B at the left, with two areas between them showing cross-stripes and vertical stripes; see bottom of the diagram.

The 'jump' forward of A at the weft crossing and that of B over the float are of course invisible on the underside of the rug, which is therefore the front in use. See Plate 6 (p. 26).

Naturally, the three boundaries between the four areas can be moved at will. If the central crossing is moved alternately to right and to left, a new area is produced between these crossing points which shows a different sort of striping.

The colours can be counter-changed from side to side if, at the end of a repeat, B is woven all across to the right selvage and then A across to the left selvage and the normal sequence resumed. It will be found that this has no effect on the cross-stripe area, but that the vertical stripes move sideways one warp end; see one quarter of the way up the sample in Plate 6 (p. 26). To counter-change the areas of vertical and horizontal stripes, as in the upper half of the sample, weft A has to take a course analogous to that of B in the diagram and vice versa.

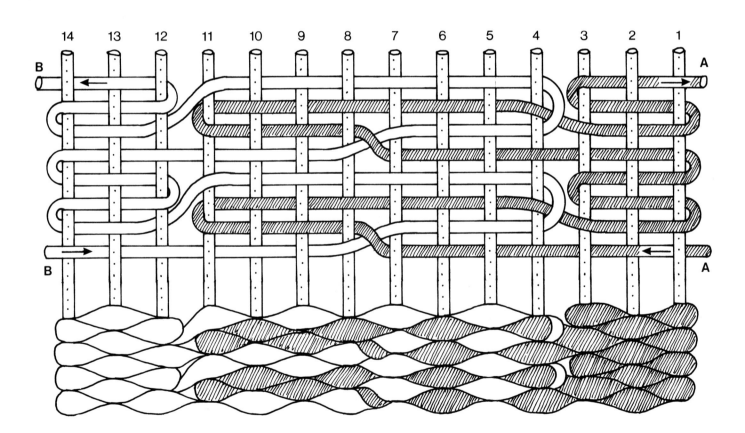

Fig.16

Weaving Inscriptions

A good way to weave letters or figures into the end of a rug is to work a band of pick-and-pick stripes and alter the colours where necessary with weft wrapping. In *Fig. 17(a)*, an **E** is imposed on such stripes. An X marks each portion which must have its colour reversed to produce the white **E** on a dark ground, seen in *Fig. 17(b)*.

Starting at the bottom, the lower arm of the **E** is made by taking the white weft out of the shed, wrapping it around end 5 and returning it into the shed, in the manner shown in *Fig. 18(b)*.

The dark weft follows in the next shed, passing normally from selvage to selvage, being hidden where the white is wrapping. The white wrapping pick is repeated to give the arm sufficient thickness; see the bottom of *Fig. 18(c)*.

Now the dark pick has to emerge from the shed and wrap around end 4, as at *Fig. 18(a)*, in order to give a solid dark area between the lower two arms of the **E**. The white weft is passed normally, being hidden by the dark wrapping. The central arm is worked exactly as the lower one, and so on.

An advantage of the method is that, if the rug is turned over, uninterrupted pick-and-pick stripes are seen instead of a mirror-image inscription as Plate 7 (p. 27) shows. It also avoids the long floats produced by the method described in TRW p. 124.

Note
— It is best if all the wrappings are in the same direction, as in (a) and (b), even though the wefts forming them may be passing in different directions. Plate 7 (p. 27) shows such an inscription at the bottom with, above it, two decorative borders using the same technique.

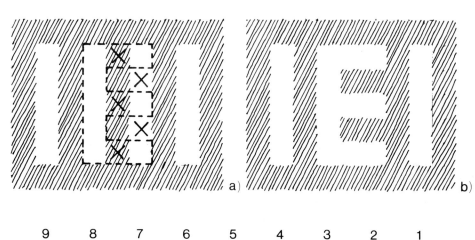

Fig.17   a)   b)

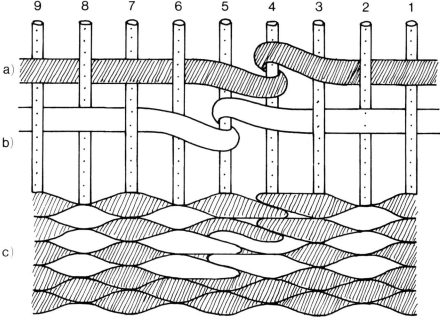

Fig.18   WEFT-FACE RUGS IN PLAIN WEAVE   **25**

Plate 6 (see p. 24)

FRONT

BACK

Plate 7 (see p. 25)

Clasped Wefts

The principle of Clasped Wefts can be applied to several different weave structures, such as plain weave, twill and the block weaves. In essence it gives picks made up of two (or more) colours, the extent to which each colour contributes to a pick being completely controllable. Wefts half the normal thickness *must* be used because, as *Fig. 19* shows, they lie doubled over in each shed.

Basic Method

Throw A (on a shuttle) from right to left, loop it around B (which can be on a ball or a cone, i.e. not on a shuttle) and then throw A back to the right selvage in the *same* shed. Pulling on A will drag a loop of B any required distance into the shed. Beat, change the shed and repeat.

The exact positioning of the clasping points between A and B is of course vital to whatever design is being woven, and is adjusted by pulling on the two free ends of weft. If, for example, the clasping points alternated regularly from side to side, as in *Fig. 19*, a rectangular central area of pick-and-pick stripes would be created, with an area of solid A on the right and of solid B on the left.

The clasping points can be treated in two ways; either located *between* two warp ends, see lower pick in diagram (making it visible from both sides of the rug, but causing no lumpiness), or carefully located *under* a raised warp end in its shed, see upper pick in diagram (making it invisible from the front, but plainly visible as a little lump on the back of the rug). The first method is obviously more suitable for a reversible floor rug; the second for a rug intended for the wall. In either case, the technical difficulty is to combine an exact positioning of the clasping point with the normal loose waving of the weft.

Though the method can be used for free designs, the following, more ordered, applications work well and show some of its many possibilities.

Using Two Wefts

Imagine the warp is divided by three lines (1, 2 and 3 in *Fig. 20*) and locate the clasping points at 1 for the first pick, at 2 for the second and at 3 for the third, and keep repeating this sequence.

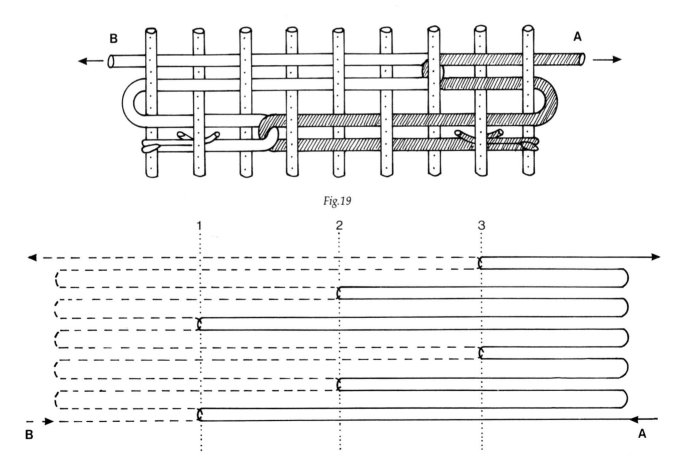

Fig.19

Fig.20

The result is an area of colour A at the right and of B at the left, with two spotted areas in between (one with spots of A on B, the other with spots of B on A); see *Fig. 20*. The spots are staggered, not arranged in vertical columns. As with all Clasped Weft techniques, the boundaries between the areas are movable. Plate 8 (p. 30) shows the result when lines 1 and 3 are inclined inwards.

In a similar way, imagine the warp divided by four lines (1, 2, 3 and 4) and locate the clasping points at 1, 2, 3 and 4 (as in *Fig. 21*) or at 1, 3, 2 and 4 (as in *Fig. 22*). The former gives

cross-stripes, the latter pick-and-pick stripes in the central area of the five areas produced. The spots in the two adjacent areas lie vertically above each other. There are areas of solid colour at both sides. Plate 9 (p. 31) shows both these possibilities.

Such regular ordering of the clasping points has many other variations, especially as different sequences can be combined and a clasping point can be located several times at one position.

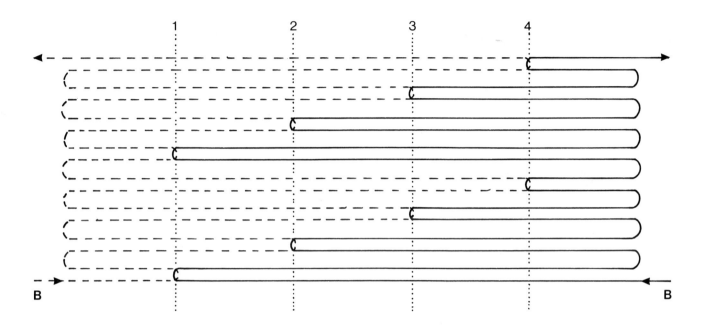

Fig.21

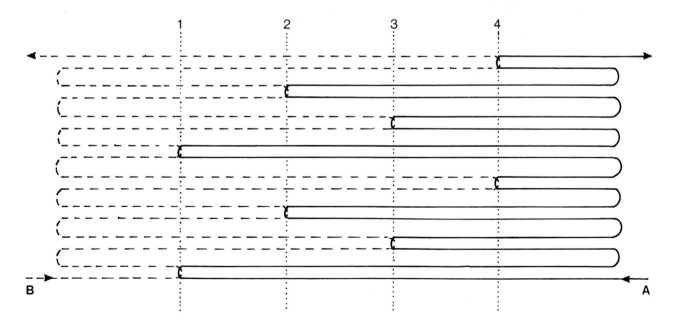

Fig.22

Plate 8 (see p. 29)

Plate 9 (see p. 29)

Using Three Wefts

With a central shuttle carrying weft A and a ball of B at the right selvage and one of colour C at the left, the possibilities multiply; see *Fig. 23*.

Enter A into the shed, pass it to the right selvage, catch it round B and pass it all across to the left selvage, pulling in a loop of B.
Adjust this right-hand clasping point and fix it with a light beat.
Then catch A round C and pass it back to the centre and out of the shed, pulling in a loop of C.
Adjust this left-hand clasping point and beat normally.
Change the shed.

The problem of entering A into the next shed without it floating over two ends is solved thus. In the previous shed, it moved first to the right; in this shed move it first to the left, carrying it around a raised warp end as it enters the shed; see the lowest small arrow in *Fig. 23*. Keep this alternation of direction going, shed by shed. To avoid the sort of weakness at the centre seen in the diagram, make the point of entry move along a diagonal or a zigzag. Alternatively the weft can occasionally leave the shed by passing under the same end it passed under on entering the shed; see the heavy arrow at top of *Fig. 23*.

This will give three areas of solid colour A, B and C. If the clasping points are moved from side to side in some regular way, there will be striped areas between these. In *Fig. 23* there will be pick-and-pick stripes between A and B, and cross-stripes between A and C. All these areas have a controllable shape; see Plate 10 (p. 34).

Using Four Wefts

One of the many ways four wefts can be handled is shown in *Fig. 24*. Shuttles carrying colours A and B lie at the left selvage, and balls of colours A and B at the right.

Throw shuttle A, pick up a loop of B at right selvage and throw it back, drawing B as far as required into the shed. Now throw shuttle B and draw a loop of A into the next shed; see first two picks in *Fig. 24*.

This will give pick-and-pick stripes of A and B at either side, with a central area which can be solid A (as at bottom of diagram) or solid B (see top pick) or any type of striping of the two colours, this area having a controllable shape; see Plate 11 (p. 35). Developments of this include using three or four colours, not just two; and using shuttle A for two picks, then B for two picks, or some such sequence, so striping other than pick-and-pick is woven at the sides.

Notes
— *A Grierson selvage is used at the left and a Navajo 1 selvage at the right.*
— *Because the wrapping of the selvage end is with half-thickness yarn, it may have to be done more times at both selvages than shown in the diagram.*
— *One incidental advantage of all Clasped Weft methods is that the yarn coming from a ball is theoretically endless, thus it never has any joins and darning-in is avoided.*

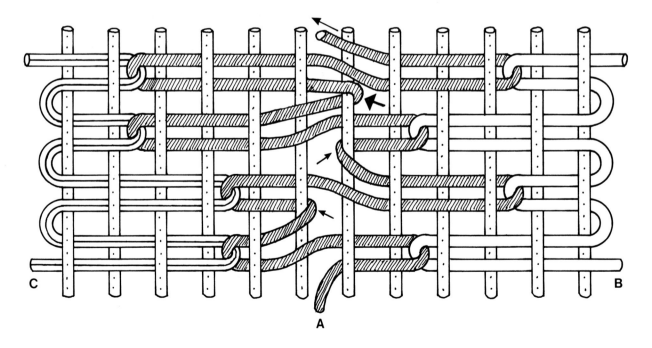

C   B

A

Fig.23

Compensated Inlay

Applying the idea of weft inlay to a weft-face textile imposes two conditions:

1. There must be two picks of the inlay weft to keep a correct shed sequence
2. The main weft must take a zigzag course as it passes from selvage to selvage in order to preserve a straight fell to the rug.

Fig. 25 shows these conditions being fulfilled and also shows that the area of inlay can be either striped (bottom) or spotted (top), depending on the presence or absence of an extra pick of the main weft. There follow some additions to the many possibilities of this technique described in TRW pp. 133–40.

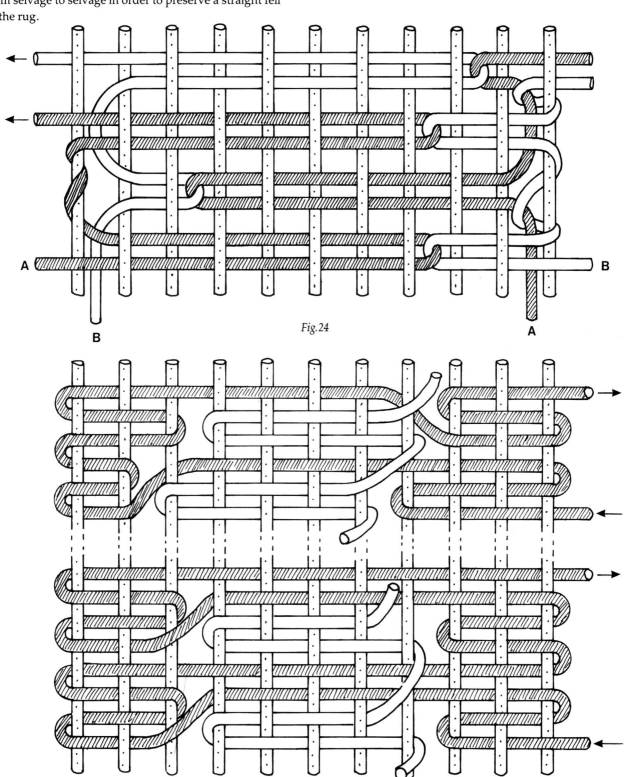

Fig. 24

Fig. 25

Plate 10 (see p. 32)

Plate 11 (see p. 32)

Striped Block with Inclined Edge

Though the 'jumps' forward from one pair of inlay wefts to the next in a striped block naturally give it a vertical edge, a convincing inclined edge can be woven as shown in *Fig. 26*; see Plate 12 (p. 38).

Working the Centre of a Block with Two Inlay Wefts

If the two wefts are not to cross each other at the centre of a block, there tends to be a weakness where they both 'jump' forward, over the main weft, to their next pick.

In a striped block this can be overcome by inclining the 'jumps' forward alternately to right and to left, as in *Fig. 27*; see Plate 13 (p. 38), bottom.

In a spotted block, one weft 'jumps' forward vertically, the left-hand one at bottom of *Fig. 28* going behind a raised warp end, and then the other weft enters the shed by going over and around the same end (number 4 in diagram). At the next repeat, roles are reversed, and the right-hand weft goes behind end 3 and the left-hand around it. This makes a good central feature when the two inlay wefts are of a different colour; see Plate 13 (p. 38), top.

If the two wefts are to cross at the centre of a striped block so that the colours change sides, the one that moves first has to float over two ends, but this is immediately tied down by the weft that moves second; see *Fig. 29*, lower crossing. If the two wefts are pushed through to the back before the main picks are woven, then crossed in a similar way as they are brought back into the appropriate shed, the crossing will now show on the back only; see top of *Fig. 29*. The first of these two possibilities was used in Plate 14 (p. 39).

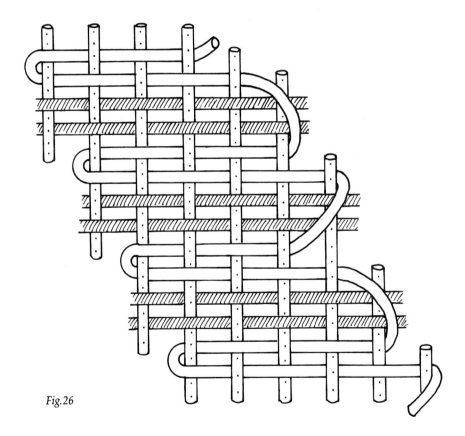

Fig.26

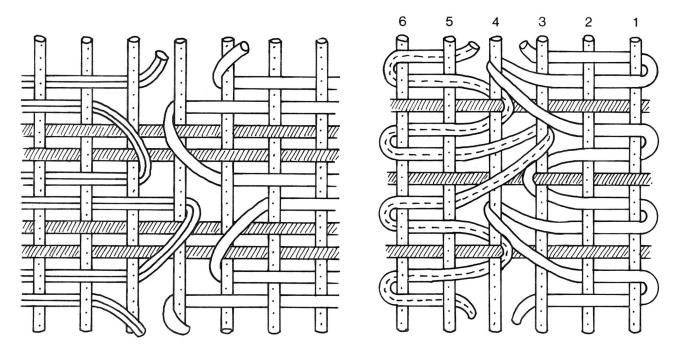

Fig. 27

Fig. 28

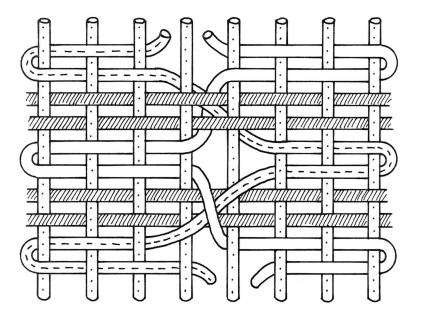

Fig. 29

Plate 12 (see p. 36)

Plate 13 (see p. 36)

Plate 14 (see p. 36)

Using Clasped Wefts for the Inlay

In another example of combining two techniques, the inlay block is woven thus:

Start with a weft of half the normal thickness at both outer edges of the block. Take one, say the right-hand, weft across the width of the block, catch it around the other weft at the left side, return to the right side dragging in a loop of this other weft, placing the clasping point where desired. Change shed and repeat this procedure. Now weave the main weft.

In *Fig. 30*, a spotted block is being woven with angled edges, so as the inlay wefts go into the next shed they both 'jump' forward over two warp ends as shown.

There are two advantages to using clasped wefts. First, the forward 'jumps' are half the normal thickness so they do not make the usual raised ridge and the rug is truly reversible. With an angled edge as described, they become part of the block and do not register as floats. Second, colour sequences not normally possible in the centre of the block are easy to work; see Plate 15 (p. 42).

Combining Spotted Blocks with Pick-and-pick Stripes

Weaving several inlay blocks, all from one weft (TRW p. 139) preceded and followed by a band of pick-and-pick stripes (as in Plate 16 on p. 42), gives yet another way of effectively combining two plain-weave techniques. *Fig. 31* shows the details. Note that there is an odd number of ends in each inlay block.

Block with Vertical Stripes

A newly worked-out form of compensated inlay disobeys the first condition laid down at the start of this section, because the inlay weft is inserted in single picks, not pairs. This gives a block of vertical pick-and-pick stripes, as in Plate 17 (p. 43). The inevitable problem of maintaining the correct shed sequence is overcome as follows:

Lay in a single pick of inlay weft, A in *Fig. 32(a)*. Between it and the selvage where the ground weft is not emerging (i.e. the right selvage in the diagram), insert a small section of ground weft, weaving with ends 1 to 4. In the diagram this has been conveniently done with the tail of the ground weft which is assumed to have started here. It could equally well have been a small separate length of ground weft.

Now, in the same shed as the inlay weft, weave the ground weft B to the right and bring it out of the shed in the same warp interspace (between raised ends 9 and 11) as the emerging inlay weft; see *Fig. 32(b)*.

Change the shed. Enter the ground weft in the new shed and carry it all the way to the right selvage, noticing that it floats over two ends, numbers 9 and 10.

Change the shed. Enter the inlay weft vertically above, so that it ties down this float and carry it as far as required by the design to the right, as in *Fig. 32(b)*.

Alternately take it over the float then *under* one warp end to the left, number 10, and then into the shed. See *Fig. 32(c)* where it is seen there is the familiar crossed weft formation. This method is neat but is visible on the back and front, whereas the first method gives one faultless surface (the back as woven) and one surface with visible 'jumps' forwards.

Fig.30

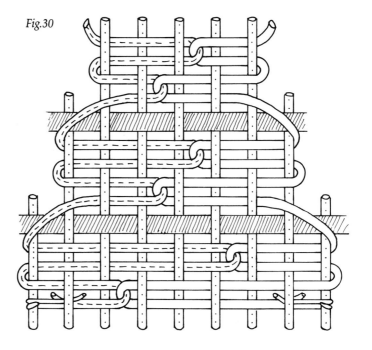

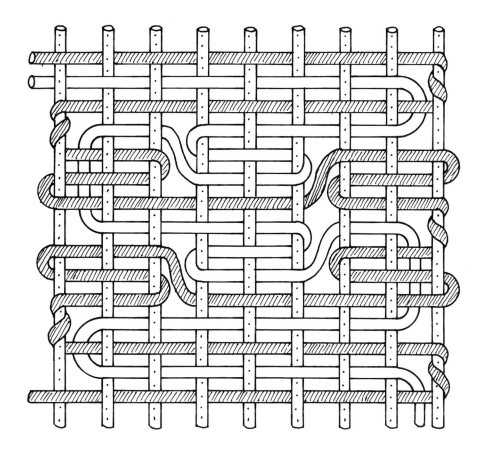

Fig.31

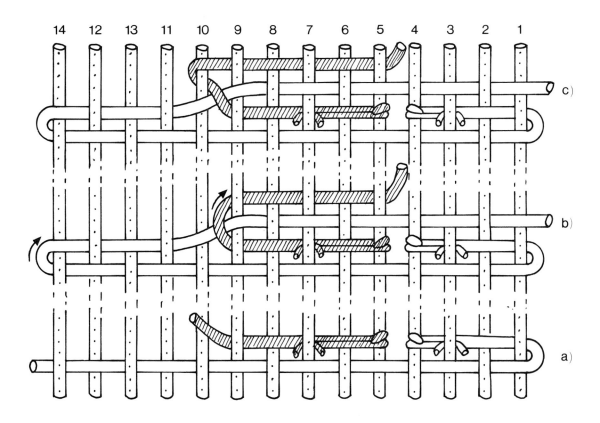

| 14 | 12 | 13 | 11 | 10 | 9 | 8 | 7 | 6 | 5 | 4 | 3 | 2 | 1 |

c)

b)

a)

Fig.32

Plate 15 (see p. 40)

Plate 16 (see p. 40)

Plate 17 (see pp. 40,44)

A similar procedure is now followed on the right: i.e. bring the ground weft up to the inlay's emerging point, change the shed and carry it to the left selvage, and so on.

To compensate for the single picks of inlay, make the ground weft take the usual zigzag course only as it starts its journey from the selvage. So its route is as shown schematically in *Fig. 33*. To avoid confusion, these compensatory picks have been omitted in the main description and diagrams.

The inlay area can be altered in size at every pick, i.e. as it moves to the right it can go as far as desired in that direction, and similarly in the next pick to the left. In Plate 17 (p. 43), it has been moved inwards or outwards after every four picks. A possible variation is to weave three inlay picks instead of one, giving a cross-stripe. This was done at the centre of the sample in Plate 17 (p. 43) and, of course, requires more compensatory picks of the ground weft.

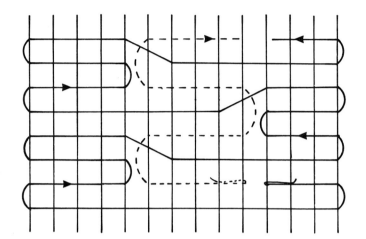

Fig.33

Combining Skip Plain Weave with Tapestry

Skip Plain Weave, in which two wefts use the same shed but pass in and out of its back layer (so where one lies *in* the shed the other *floats* at the back), is sometimes combined with tapestry weave. If the motif in *Fig. 34(a)* was woven entirely in tapestry technique, six wefts would be needed at level A – A. By using Skip Plain Weave for the narrow areas, the number is reduced to two, but with the disadvantage of having some weft floats at the back.

As *Fig. 34(b)* shows, each weft weaves normally at either side, but dives in and out of the back layer of the shed at appropriate points in the centre. Here where the dark weft lies in the shed, the white floats at the back, and vice versa. So it is only those parts heavily outlined in the diagram which will show on the surface; see the compressed view at bottom of diagram.

Pick-and-pick Stripes in Tapestry

Some Navajo rugs, from Coal Mine Mesa near Tuba City, Arizona, have triangular or rhomboidal areas of pick-and-pick stripes. The way the two alternating wefts are handled gives floats over two warp ends at one or both edges of such areas; see the left-hand edges in *Fig. 35*. The floats combine to form a slightly raised ridge, lying obliquely between adjacent areas, hence the name, 'Raised Outline', given to this style, which dates from the 1930s.

Even when an area consists of a single colour, two wefts are still used, so a ridge is produced; see the outer areas in *Fig. 35*.

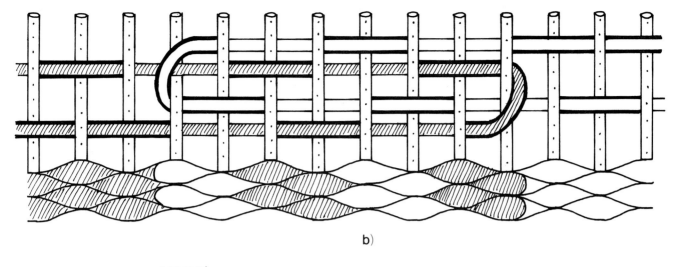

b)

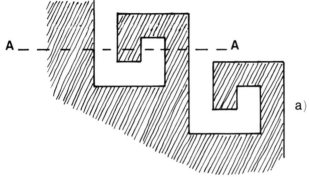

Fig.34

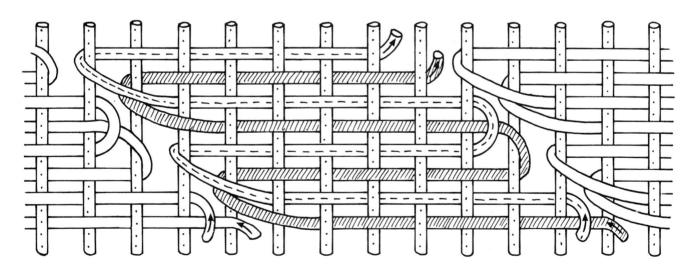

Fig.35

FRONT

BACK

WEFT-FACE RUGS IN PLAIN WEAVE   Plate 18 (see right)

Weft-face Rugs in Multishaft Weaves

Once interlacements more complex than plain weave are used for weft-face rugs, the character of the work changes. There is much less manipulation of the weft in the interests of design; it often passes without interruption from selvage to selvage. Instead, the designs result from what the shafts do to the warp, rather than what the fingers do to the weft. This greater reliance on the loom's intrinsic capabilities, on what it can give the weaver, has two linked results. There is an increase of speed when weaving, but a reduction of freedom when designing. The latter effect, though seeming a drawback, can actually become a benefit. It can stimulate ingenuity and channel the weaver into working out and weaving designs which might not otherwise have been envisaged.

Double-faced 2/1 Twill

A straight three-shaft draft, lifted for a double-faced 2/1 twill, gives a very useful rug structure. Two repeats of the draft are shown in *Fig. 36*, with a sequence of the six lifts different to the one previously given (TRW p. 260). It will be seen that each warp end stays up for three picks, then down for the next three picks.

As the odd-numbered picks (heavily outlined and shaded) show only on the front and the even-numbered only on the back, the front and back of the rug can be completely different.

The following are some possible colour sequences to use and the results they give.

1. (A,B,A,B) The rug has colour A on the front and B on the back.
2. (A,A,B,B) The rug has oblique stripes of A and B on the back and the front, the stripe lying on the opposite diagonal to that of the structural twill.

To reverse the direction of these oblique lines, the lifting sequence must naturally be read in the opposite direction, i.e. downwards instead of upwards. But to make a good transition, miss out two of the lifts.

The sequence becomes as follows, the arrows showing the reversing points:

1,12,2,23,3,13, ↓ 2,12,1,13,3,23, ↓ 1,12,2,23,3,13,

The (A,A,B,B) colour sequence continues unaltered throughout.

3. (A,A,B,B,C,C,B,B) This gives identical oblique stripes on the front and the back of the rug, a stripe of B alternating with a mixed stripe of A and C.
4. (A,B,C,A,B,C) This gives vertical stripes of the three colours on the back and the front.
5. (A,D,B,D,C,D) This gives the same vertical stripes, but only on the front, the back being solid D colour.
6. (A,C,B,C) This gives stripes of A and B on the front with solid C on the back; see Plate 18 (left).

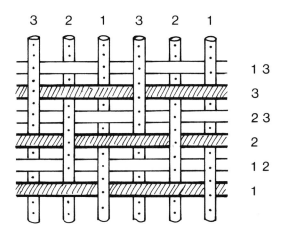

Fig.36

Practical Details

Like other three-shaft weaves, this twill presents no problems when woven on a jack or countermarch loom. The difficulty with a counterbalanced loom can be overcome by making a simple harness from two flat triangular pieces of wood; see *Fig. 37*. Each has a central hole for a suspending cord and a hole at each corner for cords running down to the three shafts. It will be understood that when any one shaft is pulled down by a pedal, the other two shafts will automatically rise, and when any two are pulled down, the other one will rise; so the six desired lifts are easily obtained. In the past, such wooden equilateral triangles, found only in Scandinavia, were thought to be for tablet-weaving.

A warp set at 4 working epi works well with a weft of 2-ply carpet wool used two-fold, i.e. a little thinner than is usual for other weaves set at 4 epi.

The wefts will not always catch naturally at the selvage in this weave, so a floating selvage should be used. The first and last end of the warp, which is probably doubled or tripled, is not threaded on a shaft but passes normally through the reed. When a shed is made, these two selvage working ends stay horizontal and do not move. The shuttle enters the shed passing over the floating selvage and leaves the shed passing under the opposite floating selvage; thus the weft always catches the outermost end at both sides. Working in this way, there will be occasional weft floats over three ends at the selvage. But because the warp ends are set a little closer at the selvage, this 3-span float is only slightly longer than the 2-span floats in the rest of the weave. If desired, however, it can be avoided by taking the shuttle under instead of over the floating selvage, or vice versa, at appropriate points in the sequence.

When using the (A,B,C) colour sequence, starting all three wefts at the same side gives a good selvage.

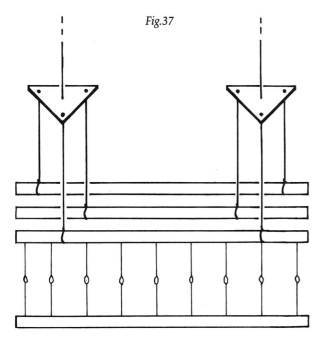

Fig.37

Using Clasped Wefts

Applying the Clasped Weft principle to this twill makes it possible to have a central block of oblique stripes with an area of solid colour on either side. *Fig. 38* shows how the three picks in the lifting sequence which appear on the front of the rug would lie. On the right is a shuttle of half-thickness weft A, on the left a ball of half-thickness weft B. The three picks appearing on the back (not shown) could be another colour altogether and, not being clasped, would, of course, be of normal thickness.

The method is worked as follows:

Lift shaft 1, throw weft A to the left going *under* the floating selvage (FS at top of *Fig. 38*), both as it enters and as it leaves the shed. Catch it around weft B and throw it back to the right, drawing a loop of A as far as required into the shed. Again it must pass under both floating selvages.

Lift shafts 12, throw normal weft for back surface of rug.

Lift shaft 2, throw A to left but this time going *over* the floating selvage both as it enters and leaves the shed, pick up a loop of B and return to the right.

Lift shafts 23, throw weft for back surface.

Lift shaft 3, throw A to left going *under* the floating selvage both as it enters and as it leaves the shed. Pick up B and return.

Lift shafts 13, throw weft for back surface.

Continue in this way, always taking A alternately over and under the floating selvages, so that the clasped wefts always catch around them at both sides, as in *Fig. 38*.

If the clasping points continue to be moved from side to side as shown, there will eventually be an area of solid B on the left, one of solid A on the right and in the centre the alternating picks of A and B will give oblique stripes; see Plate 19. (p. 50)

Naturally this central area can be any shape as its outer boundaries are dictated by the positions of the clasping points. If these are always placed under a raised warp end, the shape will have a convincing and crisp edge. The clasping points will not appear on the back of the rug, as the weft floats there will cover them. The back of the sample (see Plate 19) is solid red.

If both the front and back picks are woven with the two clasped wefts, the rug will be the same back and front, but it may be hard to conceal the large number of clasping points. If in addition the outer areas of solid colour are made as narrow as possible, this provides a simple way of weaving oblique stripes, or any other two-colour pattern in the centre, without any selvage problems. *Fig. 39* shows one way the six picks could be arranged. On both the back and the front of the rug, the central area will show oblique stripes of A and B flanked by a narrow border of solid A on the right and of solid B on the left. Plate 20 (p. 51) shows a sample based on this idea, with the colours counter-changing at the borders but the central area remaining constant.

Note
— *This twill can be woven on a warp threaded for the Three-end Block Weave. If shafts 3 and 4 are always lifted together, the block weave threading, however the blocks may be arranged, acts as a straight three-shaft draft. So the lifts become:*

$$1,12,2,23\underline{4},3\underline{4},13\underline{4}$$

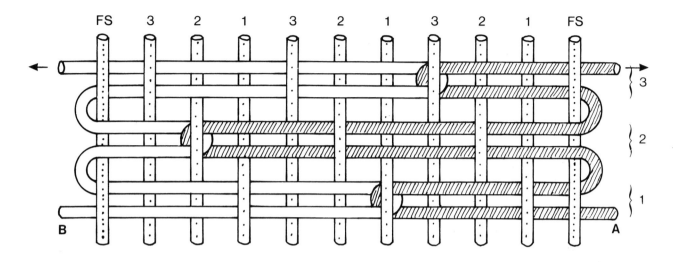

Fig.38

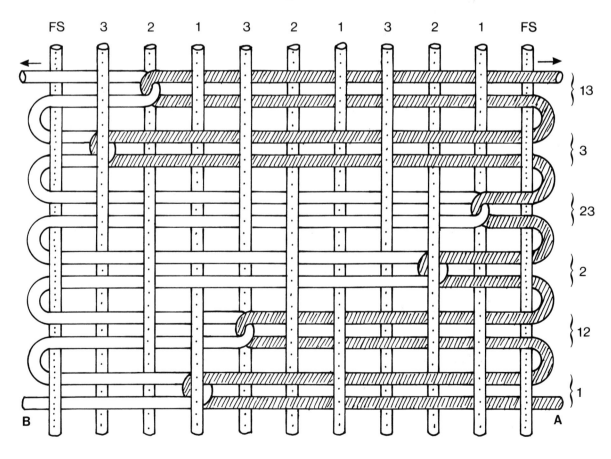

Fig.39

FRONT

BACK

                    Plate 19 (see p. 48)

Plate 20 (see p. 48)

Three-shaft Krokbragd

This rug weave has become popular because, despite its simple structure, it gives endless possibilities in design and colour combinations. *Fig. 40* shows the threading draft and the lifts. It weaves well with a warp of 4 working epi and a weft of carpet wool used two-fold. The only problem it presents is at the selvages, especially as the weft colour sequences are frequently changed. But this can be overcome by following these rules.

1. Always use *three separate wefts* (A, B and C in *Fig. 41[a]*), even if three actual colours are not needed in the design. If only two colours are needed, two of the wefts must be the same colour.
2. For each repeat of the three lifts, throw all three wefts in the *same direction*; from right to left in *Fig. 41(a)*. In the way the lifts have been arranged in *Fig. 40*, the last one thrown across is the colour which covers the selvage end, threaded on shaft 1, this is important.
3. In the next repeat, throw A and B normally, noting that they miss the selvage completely and 'jump' forward on the back; see *Fig. 41(b)*. To compensate for this, wrap weft C around the selvage end, in a downward direction, before it is thrown; see diagram. The number of wraps, perhaps two or three, should be just sufficient to create a level fell.

   This will make a perfect front to the rug. The 'jumps' forward of wefts A and B on the back will be visible, though partly hidden by the long floats of C at this point.

The right-hand selvage is handled in exactly the same manner, which, it will be seen, is really just another application of the Grierson Method for a pick-and-pick selvage.

If the selvage end is floating and not threaded on shaft 1, wefts A and B will enter and leave their sheds under the floating selvage, and weft C will leave a shed under it, wrap and then enter over it. The selvage of the three-colour part in Plate 32 (p. 67) was handled in this way.

2/2 Twill

A straight or broken 2/2 twill gives a good weft-face rug structure, which can be patterned with many more small-scale designs than are possible with the above three-shaft twill. The two sides of the rug are always identical. With a warp set at 4 working epi, a weft of 2-ply carpet wool used three-fold is suitable. This setting will make the small motifs repeat every inch across the width of the rug, as they are of necessity four warp ends wide.

To the many weft colour sequences already described (TRW pp. 272–8), the following can be added.

Straight 2/2 Twill, Lifted (12,23,34,14)

1. Nine-pick sequence: (A,A,B,B,A,A,B,A,B).
2. Twelve-pick sequence. So that the colour sequence coincides with the familiar triangular motif, start thus: (A,A,A,B,A,A,B,B,A,B,B,B). An oblique band of these triangles is seen in Plate 60 (p. 127).
3. A variant (A,A,A,B,A,A,B,A,A,B,B,B) converts the triangles into arrow shapes.
4. Using three colours in the sequence (A,A,A,B,A,A,B,B,A,B,B,B:A,A,A,C,A,A, C,C,A,C, C,C) gives a vertical row of colour A triangles, followed by a row of triangles alternately in colours B and C.

Broken 2/2 Twill, Lifted (12,23,14,34)

An interesting interlaced pattern is obtained with the sequence (A,B,A,B,A,) × 2,(A,C,A,C,A) × 2; see Plate 21 (p. 54).

All the patterns possible with three-shaft Krokbragd can be produced using various four-pick colour sequences with a broken twill. But unless a thin weft is used and beaten very hard, the colour areas are not so crisp and clean-edged. Of course, the design will be identical on both sides of the rug, unlike Krokbragd.

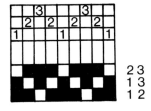

Fig.40

Skip Twills

In Skip Twills, ends in the normal straight draft (1,2,3,4) are missed (skipped) in a regular way as the shafts are threaded. Then when a known colour sequence is used, the expected pattern is sometimes elongated in the weft direction and sometimes completely altered. The same principle can be applied to the four normal lifts, skipping some in a regular order. For instance, skipping every fifth lift gives:

(12,23,34,14, 23,34,14,12, 34,14,12,23, 14,12,23,34)

or skipping every third and fourth alternately gives:

(12,23,34, 12,23, 14,12,23, 14,12, 34,14,12, 34,14, 23,34,14, 23,34).

These lifts can then be tried with any colour sequence. As an example, the first one with the twelve-pick sequence gives the expected triangles but they occur in rows leaning to one side; see Plate 22 (p. 54).

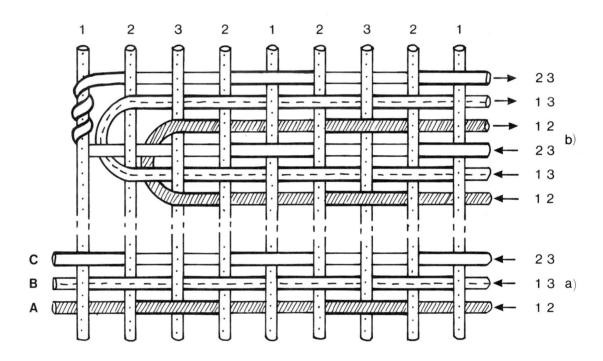

Fig.41

Plate 21 (see p. 52)

Plate 22 (see p. 53)

Plate 23 (see p. 56)

Crossed Wefts

Applying the principle of Crossed Wefts in Contrary Motion to broken 2/2 twill can give a central area of wide vertical stripes with side areas of spots vertically aligned. Two wefts start from opposite selvages, either on the 12 or the 14 lift of the broken twill sequence, and pick by pick alternate their crossing points from side to side; see *Fig. 42*. At a crossing point, always first move the weft which will float over three warp ends, not five; then move the other weft tying down this float; see *Fig. 43*. Crossing twice at one side will make the vertical stripes counter-change, giving the appearance of checks seen in Plate 23 (p. 55). The selvages give no problems, both wefts catching perfectly at both sides.

Clasped Wefts

As with the 2/1 twill above, Clasped Wefts can be used with 2/2 twills. Using half-thickness wefts, one on a shuttle at the right selvage, one on a ball at the left selvage, every pick of the straight or broken twill sequence is woven with a Clasped Weft. Thus all the two-colour patterns, which normally run from edge to edge, can be localized in the centre of the rug in an area of any desired shape, with an area of solid colour on either side.

In *Fig. 44* the clasping points for six picks have been arranged so that the colour sequence is (A,A,B) in the centre, giving thick oblique stripes of A and thin of B. If three clasping points are used, as in *Fig. 20.* (p.28) ,there will be two central areas, one with an (A,A,B), one with an (A,B,B) colour sequence, so oblique stripes of the two types can be woven side by side; see Plate 24 (p. 58).

Use a floating selvage, always taking the shuttle over it on both sides in one pick, and under it on both sides in the next pick; this gives a perfect selvage.

Unlike the 2/1 twill in which the clasping points can be hidden by the weft weaving at the back, here they will be plainly visible on the back or the front, depending how they have been placed.

The design is more convincing if the outline of the central area follows some feature in the pattern being produced, as in Plate 24 (p. 58).

Compensated Inlay

Another plain-weave technique, Compensated Inlay, works especially well with a 2/2 twill structure, giving a spotted block with an angled edge. *Fig. 45*, the general plan, shows that four picks of inlay weft is the unit, and the main weft, after taking its zigzag course from right to left, always returns to the right.

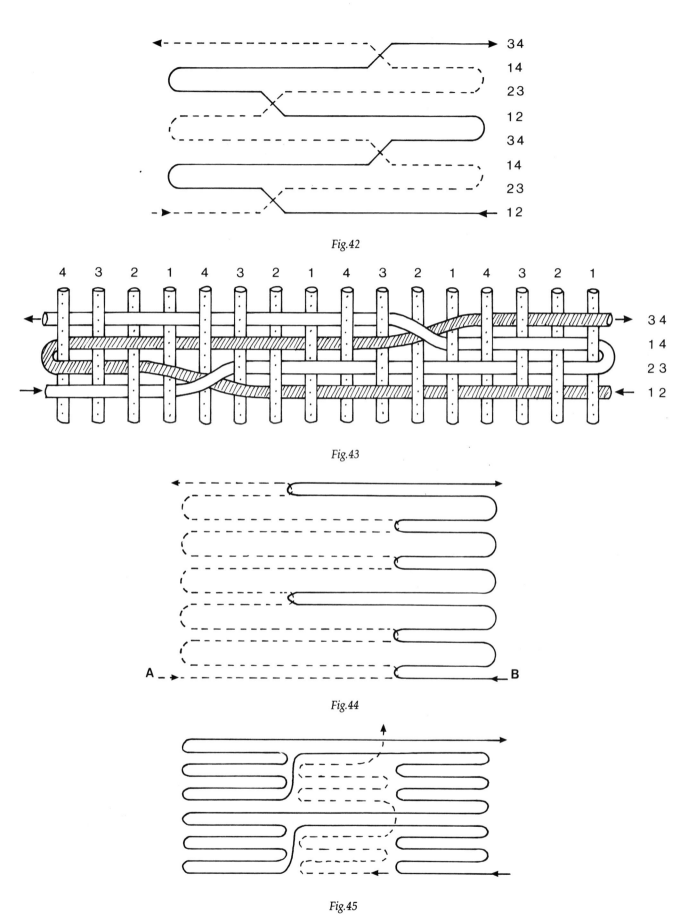

Fig.42

Fig.43

Fig.44

Fig.45

Plate 24 (see p. 56)

Plate 25 (see p. 60)

Plate 26 (see p. 60)

The method of work is as follows (see *Fig. 46)*:

Lift 12, start the inlay weft (shaded) around an end on shaft 3 and pass it to the left as far as wanted.

Lift 23, take weft around end on 3 and pass it to the right.

Lift 34, pass the weft down between the raised ends on 3 and 4, throw it to the left, bringing it up between ends on 3 and 4.

Lift 14, take the weft around end on 3, pass it to the right and bring it out between ends on 1 and 4.

Weave the main weft; first four picks at the right, allowing the weft to encroach on the warp ends used by the inlay weft to avoid a slit, as shown in diagram. Then take it across to the left selvage and weave four picks there before returning to the right. This last pick was with 23 raised, so the method proceeds thus:

Lift 34, pass the inlay weft to the left over two warp ends and over the last two picks and into the shed. The block is shifting to the left, so take it two ends further to the left, as shown. The next three picks will be exactly comparable to those in the first inlay section.

Continuing in this way, the inlay area will steadily move over to the left; see Plate 25 (p. 58). Unlike the plain weave application, the weave is quite reversible as there is no discernible 'jump' forward between one inlay section and the next. At the 'jump' forward, the weft passes over two ends exactly as does a normal weft in 2/2 twill.

Reversing the Twill Direction in a Block

The weave plan in *Fig. 47(a)* shows a 2/2 twill which in the outer areas inclines up to the left, and in the central area up to the right. This could of course be woven with a pointed draft as at *Fig. 47(b)* and with the normal (12,23,34,14) lifts. But it can be woven on a straight draft with the added advantage that the shape of the central area can be changed at will.

It will be seen that two of the picks, those when 12 and 34 are lifted (filled in black in diagram), go straight across and fit with both the twills. But for the other two picks (hatched), the shed has to be changed twice during the passage of the weft. The technique is worked as follows:

Put two markers, X and Y, in the reed to establish the boundaries of the central area.

Lift 12, pass weft A all across.

Lift 23, pass A to the first marker and take it out of the shed.

Change the shed to 14 (the opposite of 23).

Enter A and pass it to the second marker and again take it out of the shed.

Change the shed back to 23.

Enter A and pass it to the selvage.

Lift 34, pass B all across. An (A,A,B) colour sequence is being used in order that oblique colour stripes will show up the changes of twill direction.

Lift 14, pass A to the first marker and take it out of the shed.

Change the shed to 23.

Enter A and pass it to the second marker and again take it out.

Change the shed to 14.

Enter A and pass it to the selvage.

Repeat, always keeping the (A,A,B) sequence going.

Note
— *The weft always has to pass between the two raised ends of a pair, either when leaving or entering the shed at a marker. This is to avoid a float over or under four ends.*

By changing the positions of the markers the central area can increase or decrease in size or shift sideways.

Plate 26 (p. 59) shows this technique with a change to (A,B,B) colour sequence at the centre. Compare with Plate 57 (p. 122) in which the same effect is produced by shaft-switching.

Naturally the above method can be applied to other colour sequences in the weft; whatever small pattern is produced will be mirror-imaged in the central area.

2/2 Twill 'Woven on Opposites'

In this weave, each of the four normal lifts for 2/2 twill is immediately followed by the opposite lift. As *Fig. 48* shows, 12 is followed by 34, then 23 is followed by 14, and so on, giving a sequence of eight lifts. Two colours used alternately, as in *Fig. 48(a)*, will give oblique stripes of equal width; they follow the direction of the structural twill and are indeed emphasized by it. The two wefts have been shown in the weave plan and can be seen to lie on a diagonal moving up to the left, in the direction of the arrow.

Naturally the stripes can be made to lie on the other diagonal by reading the lifts in the reverse order. But almost the same effect can be obtained simply by changing the colour sequence from (A,B,A,B) to (A,B,B,A), the lifts remaining unaltered; see *Fig. 48(b)*. So here the colour stripe is running counter to the structural twill and is in fact visually not as perfect. It does mean, however, that by applying the principle of Crossed Wefts in Parallel Motion to this twill, areas striped

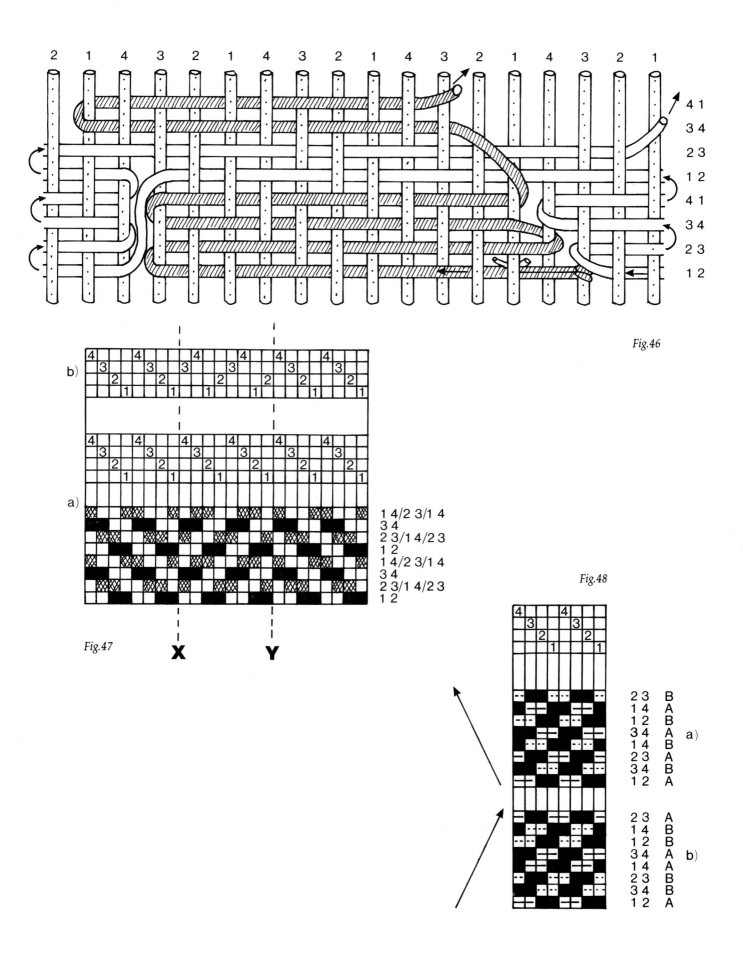

2 1 4 3 2 1 4 3 2 1 4 3 2 1 4 3 2 1

4 1
3 4
2 3
1 2
4 1
3 4
2 3
1 2

Fig.46

b)

a)

1 4/2 3/1 4
3 4
2 3/1 4/2 3
1 2
1 4/2 3/1 4
3 4
2 3/1 4/2 3
1 2

Fig.47

X   **Y**

Fig.48

2 3   B
1 4   A
1 2   B
3 4   A
1 4   B
2 3   A
3 4   B
1 2   A
a)

2 3   A
1 4   B
1 2   B
3 4   A
1 4   A
2 3   B
3 4   B
1 2   A
b)

Plate 27 (see pp. 60,64)

Plate 28 (see p. 64)

Plate 29 (see p. 64)

on the two diagonals can be woven side by side; see Plate 27 (p. 62). It is worked as follows (see *Fig. 49*):

Lift 12, throw A from right to left.

Lift 34, throw B from right to left.

Lift 23, throw A left to right only part-way, say one-third, across the warp then bring it out of the shed.

Lift 14, throw B part-way, taking it out of the shed two ends short of A's exit point. This is easy because of the way the sheds are working.

Lift 23 again, enter B into the shed, making sure it floats over four ends and bring it out another third of the way across.

Lift 14, enter A into the shed so that moving vertically it ties down the centre of the above float. Bring it out two ends short of B's exit point.

Lift 23, enter A into the shed, once more making a float over four ends, and take it all the way to the right selvage.

Lift 14, enter B into the shed so that it ties down the above float and pass it to the right selvage.

Lift 34, throw A to left.

Lift 12, throw B to left.

Lift 14 for A and 23 for B and work another two crossing picks exactly as those bracketed above, except that the points of entering and leaving the shed are of necessity moved two ends to the left or right.

Repeating these eight picks (all shown in *Fig. 49*) gives a rectangular central area whose borders are pleasantly different, because at the left crossing point it is weft B which has a long float and at the right it is weft A; see Plate 27 (p. 62).

It will be found that of the two wefts being thrown alternately one always catches the selvage thread and one always misses it but catches the next thread in. If the latter weft is allowed to miss the selvage, but the former is wrapped round the selvage thread before throwing, a very convincing one-colour selvage is produced. Unlike the similar Grierson edge, used for pick-and-pick in plain weave, there is no 'jump' forward at the back, so both sides of the rug are equally usable.

In *Fig. 50*, where there is an even number of working ends, it is weft A which misses the selvage and B which wraps at both edges. B wraps upwards when it is about to enter the shed under the selvage (see first wrap on the right); and wraps downwards when it is to enter the shed over the selvage (see first wrap on the left). Failure to follow this simple rule will produce a float over three ends. Occasionally a double wrap may be necessary to keep the fell level. Plate 28 (p. 62) shows this selvage in use with a reversal of colours where the diagonals change direction; compare with Plate 27 (p. 62) where both wefts have been caught round a floating selvage.

If the warp has an odd number of working ends, it is A which wraps (and B which misses the selvage) at one side, and B which wraps (and A which misses the selvage) at the other side. See the blue-and-white selvages in Plate 59 (p. 126).

Using Crossed Wefts in Contrary Motion with this weave gives a central area of oblique stripes with vertically aligned spots on either side. With the two wefts at opposite selvages, start with the *second* pick in the lifting sequence and make the crossings as in *Fig. 42* (p. 56). See Plate 29 (p. 63).

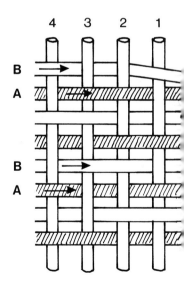

Fig.49

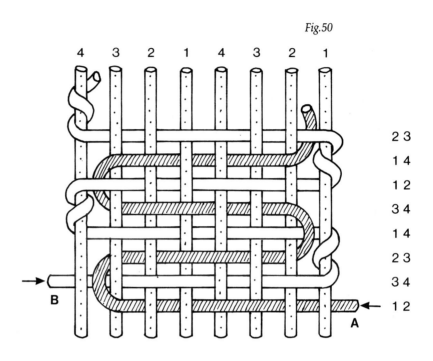

Fig.50

									2 3
									1 4
									1 2
									3 4
									1 4
									2 3
								B	3 4
								A	1 2

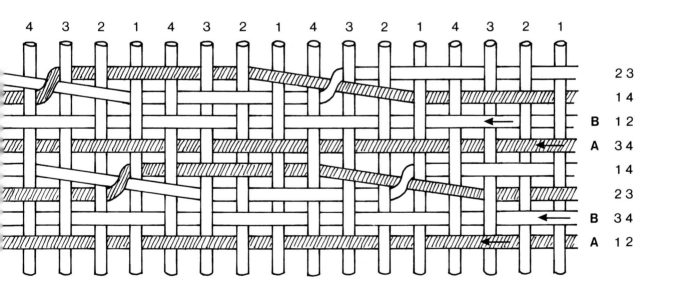

Block Weaves

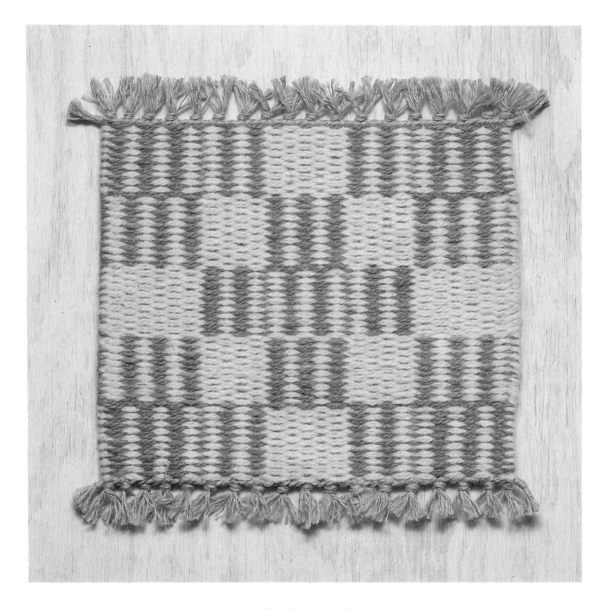

Plate 30 (see p. 68)

Plate 31 (see p. 68)

Plate 32 (see p. 68)

Three-shaft Block Weave

Four shafts are usually thought the minimum necessary for a weft-face block weave, but an interesting one can be woven on only three shafts. It uses the three possible pointed drafts, i.e. (1,2,3,2), (2,3,1,3) and (3,1,2,1). Each repeats on four ends, but if a number of repeats *plus* one end are always threaded, the three drafts will join perfectly in any sequence. *Fig. 51* shows two repeats of each draft making blocks labelled I, II and III; the linking end is circled. Of course, this I, II, III sequence is only one of several possibilities; or any two of the blocks could be used by themselves.

The plan of one possible weave is shown in *Fig. 51* and it includes all the six lifts possible with three shafts. It will be seen that each of the six picks takes a plain weave course across one of the blocks but an over 3, under 1 (or under 3, over 1) course across the other two blocks. Thus pick 1 weaves plain in Block III, but passes over 3, under 1 in Blocks I and II; pick 2 weaves plain in Block II, and passes under 3, over 1 in Blocks I and III.

When these picks are beaten in, it will be found that where the weft is weaving plain it is completely hidden by the 3-span weft floats on the front and back. The result is that only picks 1, 3 and 5 show on the front of the rug; these are marked on the diagram. There is a similar arrangement of visible colours on the back. So the colouring of the blocks is more complex than in other block weaves, any colour inevitably showing in two blocks.

The following are some of the possible colour sequences applicable to this weave.

1. (A,B,A,B) gives a rug with solid colour A on the front and B on the back.
2. (A,A,B,B) gives waving cross-stripes which do not tally exactly at the junctions *between* blocks.
3. (A,A,A,A,B,B); (B,B,A,A,A,A); (A,A,B,B,A,A). Each of these six-pick sequences, if repeated, will give one block of solid A colour, the other two blocks being striped vertically with A and B. If they are used in the given order, the block of solid A will move diagonally. If the blocks are in a I,II,III,II,I sequence, the solid A blocks will appear as a diamond, as seen in Plate 30 (p. 66), where each sequence was repeated ten times.
4. If one of the above sequences is taken and the colours counter-changed periodically, so several repeats of (B,B,A,A,A,A) would be followed by several of (A,A,B,B,B,B), solid areas of A and of B will lie above each other, flanked by striped areas, as in Plate 31 (p. 67).
5. (A,A,B,B,C,C) gives three blocks each striped with a different pair of colours.

A quite different approach is to weave this as a three-shaft Krokbragd, lifting it (12,23,13) and using a varying sequence of two or three weft colours. Small-scale patterns typical of Krokbragd will appear but will be different in each of the three blocks, as Plate 32 (p. 67) shows. If, while designing, a block is considered, what turns up in the other two can be pleasantly surprising.

As with normal Krokbragd, the back of the rug is quite different. It has simpler patterning which looks as if it were woven in plain weave.

A good warp setting is five working ends per inch, with a weft of 2-ply carpet wool used two- or three-fold. The selvage of the three-colour section at the top of Plate 32 (p. 67) was worked as shown in *Fig. 41* (p. 53).

Three-end Block Weave

In this the simplest of the four-shaft block weaves, the three-end threading units are (2,3,1) repeated ad lib, and (2,4,1) repeated ad lib. In some predetermined order, these are disposed across the width of the warp. *Fig. 52* shows a small example with only six units, threaded (2,3,1) × 2, (2,4,1,) × 2, (2,3,1) × 2, and *Fig. 53* shows the corresponding thread diagram.

The shafts are lifted in the sequence (13,14,23,24) with an (A,B,A,B) colour sequence. This causes each weft partly to weave over 2, under 1, and so show on the front, and partly to weave under 2, over 1, and so show on the back of the rug. Taking the first pick as an example, A (dark) passes under 2, over 1 in the two outer blocks threaded (2,3,1), so will appear on the back. But in the central block threaded (2,4,1), it passes over 2, under 1 and so will appear on the front.

Pick 2, white, does exactly the opposite, appearing on the front in the outer blocks and on the back in the centre. When beaten these two picks slide over each other in such a way that the white is the only colour visible in the outer blocks, and the dark in the centre; i.e. the parts heavily outlined slide over and cover the parts marked with crosses.

Picks 3 and 4 are similar but with their floats shifted one end to right or left and when beaten they slide over each other in the same way.

When this sequence of four picks is repeated several times, blocks will begin to appear as at the bottom of *Fig. 53*. Thus the position of the blocks depends entirely on how the warp is threaded; once this is done, the blocks are fixed. See Plates 33 and 34 (pp. 70–1) which show the two sides of a sample.

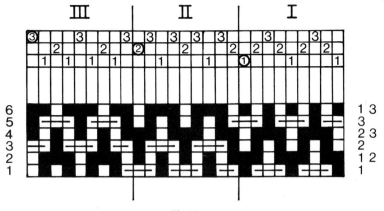

Fig.51

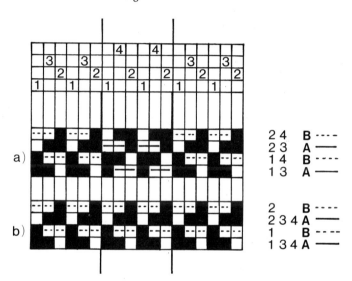

Fig.52

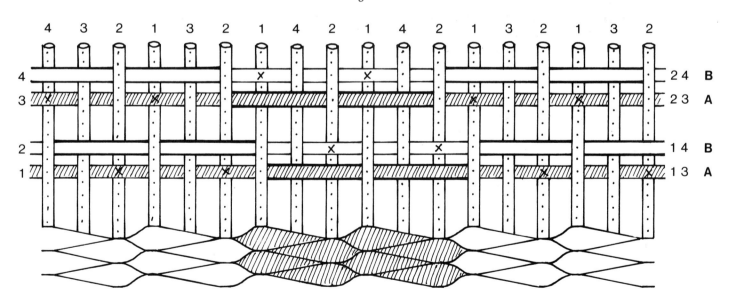

Fig.53

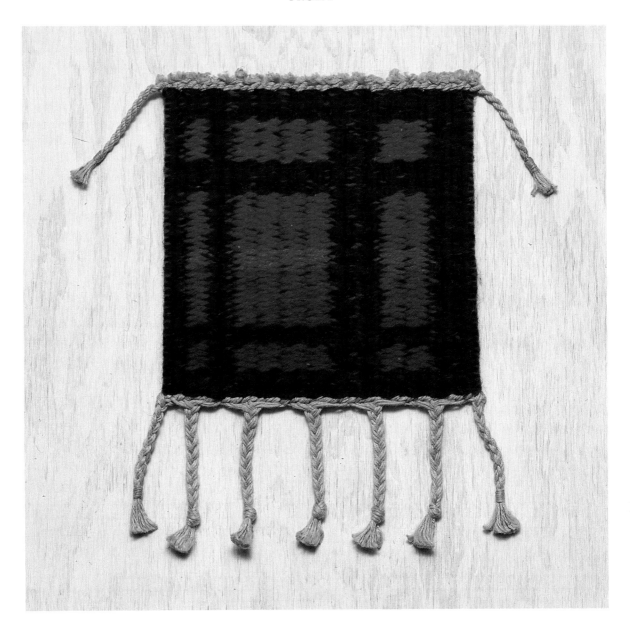

Plate 33 (see pp. 72-3)

Plate 34 (see pp. 72-3)

Practical Details

Threading Warp

A setting of 4 working epi is ideal. So if the warp consists of 6 epi on the beam, it has to be threaded alternately single, double in the heddles (starting and finishing with a triple selvage thread), and sleyed similarly. Using the threading described, the selvages catch perfectly when two shuttles are thrown alternately. But to accommodate all variations of the technique, it is best to have the outermost thread at each side as an adjustable floating selvage; see *Fig. 54(a)*.

Leave an empty heddle on shaft 4 beside every filled heddle on shaft 3, and an empty heddle on 3 beside every filled heddle on 4, as shown. This is done for two reasons: first, so that with a long warp, the position of the blocks can easily be changed after each rug is woven and cut off; second, so that the warp set-up is ready for later conversion to shaft-switching if required.

The threading unit therefore needs four heddles (one on each shaft), of which three carry warp ends and one is left empty. All these details are seen in *Fig. 54(a)* which shows the first two, right-hand, units and the final unit on the left of a rug warp.

An 8 dents/inch reed with thick wires works well and is sleyed as shown in *Fig. 54(b)*.

Weft

A 2-ply carpet wool used three-fold – or yarn of similar thickness – is suitable.

Heading

As no plain weave is possible, weave the heading with a lifting sequence of (13,24,14,23). This uses the two pairs of opposite lifts and opens the warp out satisfactorily. One shuttle carrying a very heavy yarn can be used and it will catch at both selvages, due to the alternation of 1 and 2 in the lifts.

Starting to Weave

One or two rows of weft twining is desirable before the rug proper begins, as it makes a better structure against which to work a rug finish than the block weave itself.

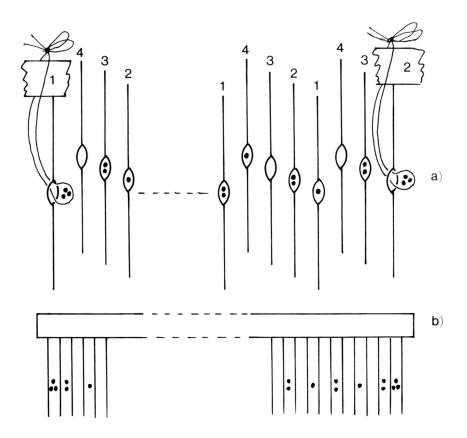

a)

b)

Fig.54

The two wefts, A and B, can either both start from the same side, or A, say, from the right and B from the left. There is always a tendency for a weft, which should be confined to the back, to show slightly on the front and vice versa; X in *Fig. 53* marks the points where this can occur, an effect obviously more apparent if A and B differ greatly in depth or hue. Now if A and B are started from opposite sides and each pick is beaten in separately, these little spots of colour will be seen. But if they are started from the same side, they can easily be waved together and then beaten together. The spots will then be eliminated because by this means the wefts have a better chance of sliding one behind the other.

Whichever shuttle is weaving the colour showing on the outermost block should always lie in front of the other shuttle during weaving. This ensures that the wefts take the neatest route as they enter each shed.

Weaving Blocks

The lifts to make the blocks appear are (13,14,23,24) with the two wefts alternating.

There are two ways of counter-changing the colours in the blocks.

1. Change the colour sequence to (B,A,B,A), but keep the lifting sequence unchanged. So it becomes 13,B; 14,A; 23,B; 24,A.
2. Change the lifting sequence to (14,13,24,23), but keep the colour sequence unchanged. So it becomes 14,A; 13,B; 24,A; 23,B.

Weaving a Solid Colour all Across

If a solid colour all across is wanted, the shafts can be lifted as for the blocks but using two shuttles alternately, *both* of which carry the same colour. Two shuttles are used to ensure that the weft catches both selvages. The back and front of the rug will then show one colour all across.

Alternatively, the two-colour weft sequence (A,B,A,B) can be maintained, but the lifts altered to (134,1,234,2), as shown in *Fig. 52(b)*. The rug will then have colour B all across on the front and colour A on the back. See the areas between the blocks in Plates 33 and 34 (pp. 70–1).

Note
— *Before moving from one of these sequences to the other, always complete the four lifts.*

Plate 35 (see right)

FRONT

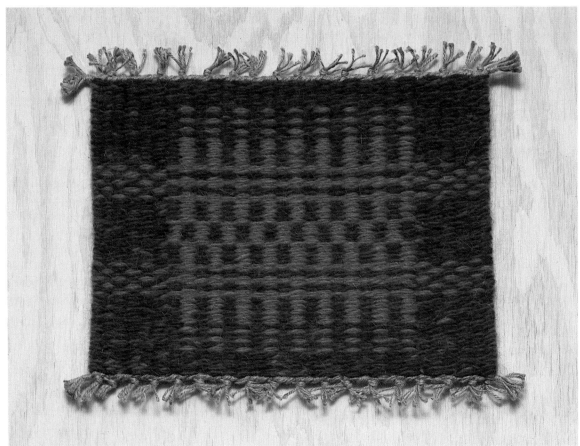

BACK

Plate 36 (see right)

Weaving Stripes and Spots

Much variety can be introduced into the blocks by turning them from areas of solid colour into areas of spots and weft- and warpway stripes. See Plates 35 and 36 (left).

Fig. 55 is a table of the two-colour variations. These are shown in diagrammatic form down the centre of the table; to the left of the midline they are in the blocks threaded on (2,4,1), to the right of the midline in the blocks threaded on (2,3,1). All the variations can be produced in two quite different ways.

1. Constant Colour Method. The colour sequence (A,B,A,B) remains unaltered but the lifts are changed. These lifts are shown on the left of each variation.
2. Constant Lift Method. The lifts (13,14,23,24) remain unaltered, but the colour sequences are changed. These are shown on the right of each variation.

Usually the first way is the easier to weave as there are never the selvage problems encountered in the second method. But it does involve the use of eight different lifts (all those shown in *Fig. 52[a]* and *[b]* in various combinations), instead of only four.

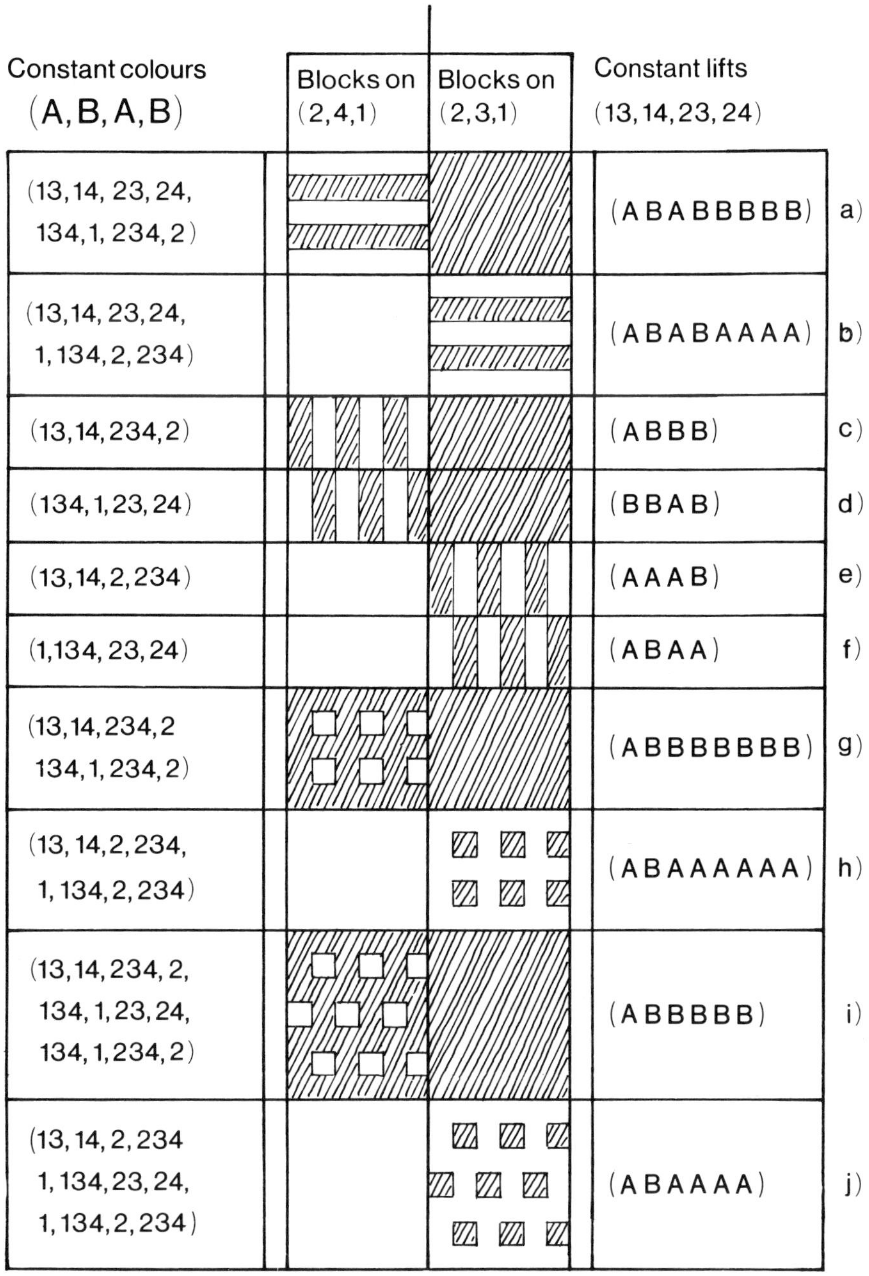

Constant colours (A,B,A,B)	Blocks on (2,4,1)	Blocks on (2,3,1)	Constant lifts (13,14,23,24)	
(13,14,23,24, 134,1,234,2)	weftway stripe	weftway stripe	(ABABBBBB)	a)
(13,14,23,24, 1,134,2,234)		weftway stripe	(ABABAAAA)	b)
(13,14,234,2)	warpway stripe	warpway stripe	(ABBB)	c)
(134,1,23,24)	warpway stripe	warpway stripe	(BBAB)	d)
(13,14,2,234)		warpway stripe	(AAAB)	e)
(1,134,23,24)		warpway stripe	(ABAA)	f)
(13,14,234,2 134,1,234,2)	spots		(ABBBBBBB)	g)
(13,14,2,234, 1,134,2,234)		spots	(ABAAAAAA)	h)
(13,14,234,2, 134,1,23,24, 134,1,234,2)	spots		(ABBBBB)	i)
(13,14,2,234 1,134,23,24, 1,134,2,234)		spots	(ABAAAA)	j)

Fig.55

Weftway stripes

See *Fig. 55(a)* and *(b)*. The instructions given in the table will give the narrowest possible stripes; these can be widened by repeating the first or second half of the sequence as often as wished.

Warpway stripes

See *Fig. 55(c)* to *(f)*. These are produced by making the two wefts surface alternately in the chosen block. They beat down to make narrow stripes in the warp direction (see top of *Fig. 56*), comparable to pick-and-pick stripes in plain weave. The stripes can be made to shift one end sideways, as shown; compare *(c)* with *(d)*, and *(e)* with *(f)*. This small manoeuvre is useful in a rug design as it helps disguise the fact that the stripes can never be centred exactly on a block.

Spots

See *Fig. 55 (g)* to *(j)*. Spots can either be aligned in vertical columns, see *(g)* and *(h)*, or staggered, see *(i)* and *(j)*, also *Fig. 56* at bottom. They are produced by alternating one of the sequences for warpway stripes with those for solid colour all across. In this way the two wefts surfacing in a block will either be in a (A,B,B,B) or (A,B,B) sequence.

When weaving stripes and spots using the Constant Colour method, the back is an exact reverse of the front; wherever A shows on the front B shows in the identical place on the back; compare Plates 35 and 36 (p. 74). Using the Constant Lift method, it is the blocks themselves which are reversed on the back, not the individual colours; compare Plates 38 and 39 (p. 79).

To make warpway stripes all across the rug, lift (134,1, 234,2) with a (B,A,A,B) or a (A,B,B,A) colour sequence.

Combinations

Obviously these features can be combined; for instance there could be spots in the blocks threaded (2,3,1) and cross-stripes in the blocks threaded (2,4,1). To work out such a combination, a basic fact has to be understood.

A weft inserted when 1$\underline{3}$ or 2$\underline{3}$ is lifted appears in the blocks threaded (2,$\underline{4}$,1); and a weft inserted when 1$\underline{4}$ or 2$\underline{4}$ is lifted appears in the blocks threaded (2,$\underline{3}$,1).

Using the Constant Lift method, write out the lifts several times. Then over the 1$\underline{3}$s and 2$\underline{3}$s (because the stripes are wanted in the 2,$\underline{4}$,1 blocks) write a colour sequence which will give stripes, e.g. A,A,A,B,B,B. Then under the 1$\underline{4}$s and 2$\underline{4}$s write a sequence which will give spots, e.g. A,B,B for staggered spots. So it now looks like this:

$$
\begin{array}{cccccc}
\text{A} & \text{A} & \text{A} & \text{B} & \text{B} & \text{B} \\
1\underline{3}, & 1\underline{4}, & 2\underline{3}, & 2\underline{4}, & 1\underline{3}, & 1\underline{4}, & 2\underline{3}, & 2\underline{4}, & 1\underline{3}, & 1\underline{4}, & 2\underline{3}, & 2\underline{4}, \\
\text{A} & \text{B} & \text{B} & \text{A} & \text{B} & \text{B}
\end{array}
$$

Combining these two into (A,A,A,B,A,B,B,A,B,B,B,B) and weaving this unlikely-looking colour sequence will give the desired result. There will of course be selvage problems, necessitating a floating selvage. Though woven by the Constant Colour method, Plate 35 (p. 74) shows in two places a comparable combination of spots and stripes as just described.

By the same reasoning it can be worked out that in order to weave the type of interlacing pattern seen in *Fig. 57*, the colour sequences are:

(A,A,B,A) × 2, (A,B,B,B) × 2, for one step in the design and (A,A,A,B) × 2, (B,A,B,B) × 2 for the next step. See Plate 37 (p. 78) for the woven result.

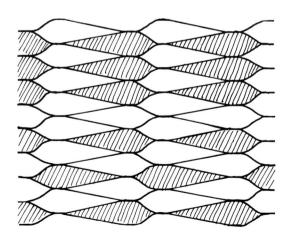

Fig.56

Fig.57

Using Three Colours

The introduction of a third weft colour means that a block can show stripes or spots in two colours and be flanked by blocks of a third colour. These variations are best worked in the Constant Lift method, all the effects coming from the different sequences of the three colours. *Fig. 58* presents a table of some of the possibilities, most of which are seen in Plate 38 (p. 79).

The cross-stripes in (*a*) and (*b*) present no difficulties, but the warpway stripes, (*c*) to (*f*), all give selvage problems. The weaving of (*c*) will be described in detail to illustrate how these problems can be dealt with.

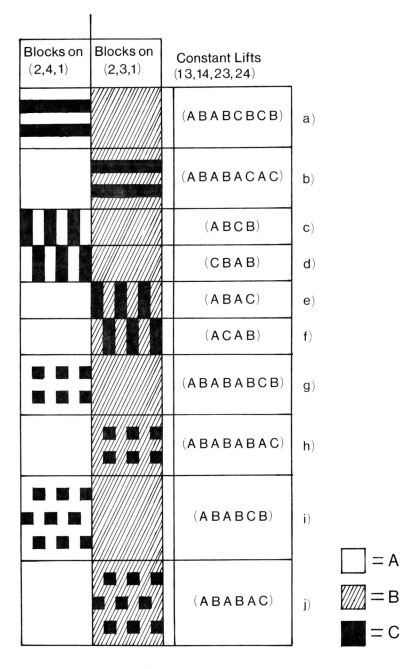

Fig.58

Plate 37 (see p. 76)

Plate 38 (see pp. 76,77,80)

Plate 39 (see p. 76)

Start with weft B at the left selvage, and wefts A and C both at the right; see *Fig. 59* (for the sake of clarity, B is not shown. It weaves normally throughout).

Lift 13, pass A *under* the selvage end (which is down) and up into the shed, forming a float under three ends.

Lift 14, throw B to the right.

Lift 23, bring C *up* between the two outermost ends (on shafts 2 and 3), thus tying down the above float, and throw it to the left.

Lift 24, throw B to the left.

All three wefts are now at the left selvage.

Lift 13, pass A *over* the selvage end and down into the shed.

Lift 14, throw B to the right.

Lift 23, pass C *down* between the two outermost ends and then into the shed. It forms a float under three ends which is already tied down by the last pick of A.

Lift 24, throw B to the left.

The wefts are back at their starting positions and the above eight picks can be repeated. *Fig. 59* shows how A and C behave at the selvage; they cross in a way similar to that in the pick-and-pick selvage using the Navajo Method 2.

Note
— With all the possibilities shown in Fig. 58, *a block can display any of the small-scale two-colour patterns obtained with plain weave, but here they are in a specific area surrounded by a third colour, as Plate 38 (p. 79) shows.*

Combinations

Applying the principle described for two colours, it is possible to work out a colour sequence which will give, say, aligned spots in one block (with an A,A,A,B sequence) with cross-stripes in the alternate block (with a C,C,B,B sequence). This gives the following: (A,C,A,C,A,B,B,B). The idea can of course be extended to include four colours, so each block is completely different in both colouring and patterning.

Other Ways of Weaving Three-end Block Weave

1. The order of the four lifts in either sequence in *Fig. 52* can be altered so that for a solid colour it becomes (134,234,2,1), and for the blocks (13,23,24,14). In both cases the colour sequence must also change to (A,A,B,B). The appearance is slightly different, with the underside weft tending to show more on the front. This sequence is used to advantage in the pick-up version of this block weave.
2. Lifting as for the heading, i.e. (13,24,14,23), with a colour sequence of (A,B,A,B,B,A,B,A) gives small oblique lines in the blocks threaded on (2,3,1) and zigzag cross-stripes in the other blocks. The blocks can be counter-changed by lifting (24,13,23,14) or (14,23,13,24), in both cases using the above colour sequence. The latter lifts were used in Plate 40 (p. 82) and this kept the oblique lines running on the same diagonal in all the blocks.
3. Lifting as for a 2/2 twill, (12,23,34,14), with a colour sequence of (A,A,B,B) gives solid colour in the blocks on (2,3,1) and vertical stripes in the other blocks. So it is similar to *Fig. 55 (e)* and *(f)*. The blocks are counter-changed with an (A,B,B,A) sequence; whereas a (A,B,A,B) sequence gives vertical stripes all across.

Varying the Appearance of the Blocks

1. Varying the blend of colours. As the weft is usually a yarn used two- or three-fold, there is every opportunity for winding several colours together on one or both shuttles and for changing these colours subtly or suddenly in the course of weaving a block, as seen in Plate 33 (p. 70).

1　3　2　1　3　2

→ C 2 3
→ A 1 3

2 3
1 3

C ---→
A ---→

Fig.59

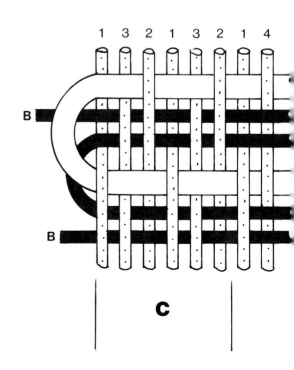

1　3　2　1　3　2　1　4

B

B

C

A block can be made less obvious if it shares a colour with the adjacent blocks. For instance, one shuttle could carry two red and one black yarns and the other shuttle carry three blacks.

2. A similar effect is obtained if one shuttle carries a tie-dyed weft. If it is space-dyed red and black and the other shuttle is all black, then the block will appear or disappear depending on whether or not the red part of the weft happens to coincide with the position of a block.

3. Two wefts of quite different texture but the same colour, e.g. white brushed mohair and white carpet wool, will give blocks differing only in their surface texture; see Plate 41 (p. 83). The more similar the two textures, the larger the blocks must be in order to register visually.

4. Very subtle blocks can be obtained by using two wefts of the same colour, but one in an S-plied the other in a Z-plied form.

Clasped Wefts

The methods described so far introduce variety into the blocks, but all the blocks across the rug which are threaded similarly of necessity look the same. This sameness can be overcome by introducing the Clasped Weft principle.

Fig. 60 shows the set-up at its simplest with a warp

threaded for five blocks. At the right selvage is a shuttle carrying weft C of normal thickness; this will form the background blocks, threaded on (2,3,1). Also at the right selvage there is another shuttle with weft A which is wound on at half the normal thickness. At the left selvage is a ball (or cone or spool) of weft B, also of half normal thickness. The work proceeds as follows:

Lift 13, throw shuttle with weft A to the left selvage, catch it round weft B and throw it back to the right, pulling a loop of B into the shed. Adjust the clasping point so it lies behind a raised warp end, as shown in the detailed *Fig. 61*.

Lift 14, throw weft C to the left.

Lift 23, throw A as before picking up a loop of B. Again locate the clasping point behind a raised end.

Lift 24, throw C back to the right.

Repeating these four picks, shown in *Fig. 61*, will make the right-hand block threaded (2,4,1) colour A, and the left-hand one colour B. This effect will be obtained as long as the clasping points are *somewhere* in the central block; their exact position being immaterial as wefts A and B are here hidden by weft C. In *Fig. 60* and subsequently, the clasping points are marked by circles, sometimes numbered to clarify their sequence. Naturally the clasping points will be visible on the back of the rug, so this is really a one-sided technique.

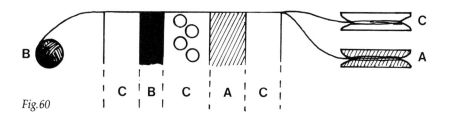

Fig.60

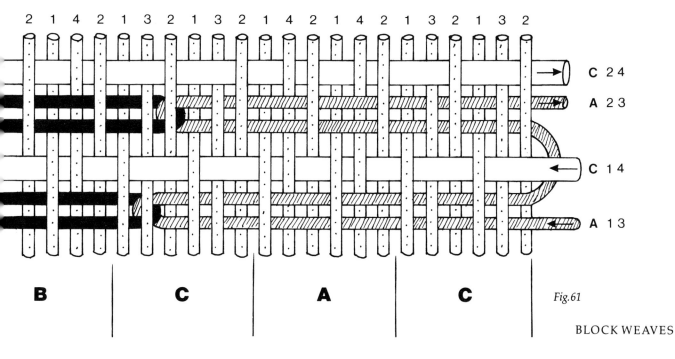

B   C   A   C   Fig.61

Plate 40 (see p. 80)

Plate 41 (see p. 81)

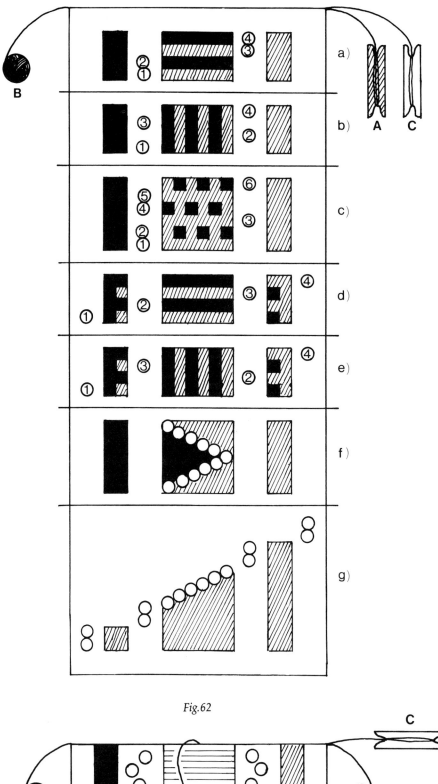

Fig.62

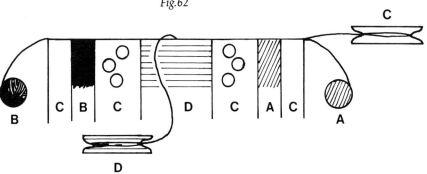

Fig.63

Fig. 62(a), (b) and *(c)* show in a diagrammatic way how moving the clasping points makes it possible to produce blocks with horizontal and vertical stripes and spots. So in *(a)*, the clasping point is twice on the left side, twice on the right of the central block giving it the narrowest possible cross-stripes. In *(b)*, the clasping points alternate from side to side of the central block giving it vertical stripes. In *(c)*, the clasping point is twice (it could be three times) to the left, once to the right of the central block, giving it staggered spots. These stripes and spots are seen in the central block in Plate 42 (p. 86).

In these three examples the two outer blocks remain a solid colour, but by moving the clasping points about more freely the outer blocks can, for instance, be spotted. This will happen if they are placed as in *(d)* or *(e)*; see bottom of Plate 42 (p. 86).

In all the above examples the clasping point has been carefully hidden between blocks threaded on (2,4,1); but if it is placed within such a block, the latter will be partly colour A, partly B. The idea works well if the clasping point is made to move diagonally. So it is placed under the next raised end – to the right, if the diagonal is moving up to the right – and a convincing oblique colour junction is produced; see *Fig. 62(f)*, and Plate 43 (p. 86). In this case the clasping points are not seen on the front or back. A colour junction with a steeper angle results from moving the clasping point over one warp end (whether raised or lowered in the shed), and allowing it to be visible.

There are other possibilities:

(a) Two balls of different colour at the left selvage

Weft A can catch either of these colours as desired. The selvage works best if one is caught for two picks, then the other for two picks.

(b) Weft at left selvage the same colour as weft C

Blocks can be made to disappear if the ball of half-thickness yarn at the left selvage is the same colour as the full thickness weft C. *Fig. 62(g)* shows where the clasping points must be for a block to disappear suddenly (outer two blocks) or gradually (central block). See Plate 44 (p. 87), where the clasped wefts changed sides at the midpoint of the sample.

(c) Ball at either selvage, shuttle in the centre

This is very like the plain weave application (see *Fig. 23* on p. 32), except that, due to the weave structure, the central 'jump' forward is handled differently. It gives the possibility of three blocks all of different colours; see *Fig. 63*. A shuttle of half-thickness D operates from the middle of the central block, and balls of half-thickness A and B are at the right and left selvages respectively. Weft C is of normal thickness.

Lift 13, pass D to right selvage, catch it around A, throw it all the way to left selvage (dragging a loop of A into the shed), catch it around B and throw it back to the middle of the warp. There it leaves the shed under the same end it passes under on entering; see detailed *Fig. 64*.

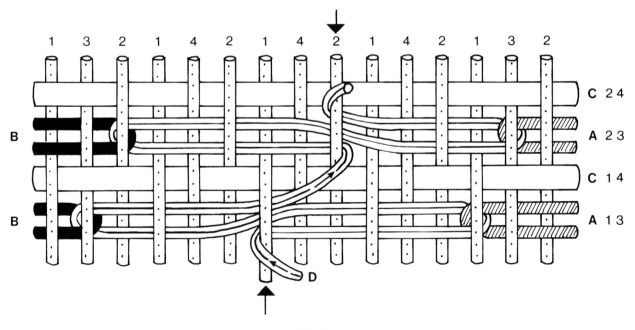

Fig.64

Plate 42 (see p. 85)

Plate 43 (see p. 85)

Plate 44 (see p. 85)

Lift 14, throw C to the left.

Lift 23. The last pick of D started by going to the right. This one goes first to the left, entering the shed around a raised end to the right (see arrow at top of diagram). After catching weft B then A, it returns to the centre and emerges under the same arrowed end.

Lift 24, throw C to the right.

Fig. 64 shows these four picks in detail, but for simplicity it includes only the central block and a portion of the two flanking blocks.

This is the whole repeat; D starting alternately to right and to left in order to make a neat central 'jump' forwards. So the next repeat begins on 13 with D going first to the right around the nearest raised warp end to the left (lower arrow), and so on. Plate 45 (p. 90) shows this technique with the half-thickness wefts A,B and D changing places regularly to give a diagonal movement to these colours.

By placing the clasping points within the blocks as well as between them, a design such as the one shown in *Fig. 65* can be woven in which it is assumed that the two balls at the selvages are of the same colour.

(d) Using four half-thickness wefts

For this interesting variation, there is a shuttle at each selvage, one carrying colour A, the other B; and there is also a ball at each selvage, both of the same colour C. All are half normal thickness; no normal weft is used, because all picks consist of clasped wefts. *Fig. 66* shows this set-up. The work proceeds as follows:

Lift 13, throw A to the left, catch it around C, throw it back, drawing a loop of C into the shed.

Lift 14, throw B to the right, catch it around C, throw it back to the left, drawing a loop of C into the shed.

Lift 23, as for 13.

Lift 24, as for 14.

All the wefts catch perfectly at the selvages.

This is a confusing technique to design for; the appearance of *any* colour both in a block threaded (2,3,1) and in a block threaded (2,4,1) is partly controlled by the weave structure and partly by the placing of the clasping point. To take a very simple example, assume the right half of the warp in *Fig. 66* is threaded (2,3,1) and the left half (2,4,1). Then when 13 or 23 are lifted, colour A can show only in the area threaded (2,4,1), i.e. the left half of the warp. Similar restrictions apply when 14 or 24 are lifted. So the left half can show various arrangements of A and C, and the right half arrangements of B and C, as suggested in *Fig. 66*, which omits the positions of the clasping points.

(e) Two balls of different colour at left, two shuttles of different colour at right selvage

In this variation the four half-thickness wefts for the block always work in pairs. In Plate 46 (p. 91), the red-and-blue weave for two repeats always clasping at the centre of the block; then the black-and-white weave for two repeats with a clasping point which gradually moves diagonally across the block. A fifth weft of normal thickness provides the background colour.

There are probably many other ways clasped wefts can be used in conjunction with the three-end block weave, some being very slow to weave.

Dovetailing

A good way to introduce two colours into a block is to apply the dovetailing principle found in tapestry. Three shuttles are needed carrying wefts A,B and C of normal thickness; see *Fig. 67* which shows a warp with one central block. The technique is worked as follows:

Lift 13, throw A from the right selvage and B from the left. Bring them both out of the shed at the same spot, somewhere in the central block.

Lift 14, throw C to the left.

Lift 23. Now, as A and B are inserted into this shed and return to their own selvages, they must both go around the same raised warp end (arrowed at top of the detailed diagram, *Fig. 68*). This is the dovetailing; to its right the block will be colour A, to its left colour B.

Lift 24, throw C back to the right.

Obviously, if this dovetail continued in the same place, it would cause a surface ridge; so it is advisable to move it up on an angle, or stagger it from side to side. To make a clean colour junction on the diagonal going up to the right, work as described above. For a colour junction on the opposite diagonal, A and B must move inwards, towards each other, on the 23 lift (not the 13 lift as above). To get into this situation, simply weave two picks of any one of the three wefts on 13 and 14, then bring in A and B on 23. This will give small spots of whichever colour weft was used, as seen in Plate 47 (p. 94).

This method has an advantage over clasped wefts in that the dovetailing is far less of a surface imperfection than a clasping point. But it can be used with ease only at a point where the wefts are showing on the surface, i.e. in a block threaded (2,4,1) in this example. To dovetail two wefts where they are appearing on the back, i.e. in a (2,3,1) block, is a finicky operation.

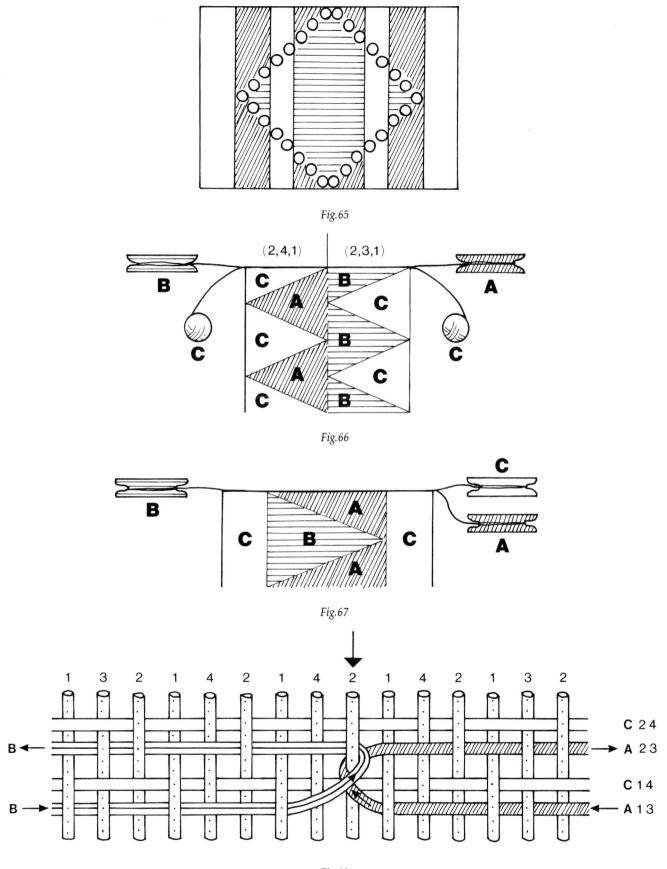

Fig.65

(2,4,1)   (2,3,1)

B   C   A   B   C

C   C   B   C

C   A   B   B

C   B

Fig.66

B   C   B   A   C

              A

Fig.67

1 3 2 1 4 2 1 4 2 1 4 2 1 3 2

C 24

B ←   → A 23

C 14

B →   ← A 13

Fig.68

Plate 45 (see p. 88)

Plate 46 (see p. 88)

Pick-up Version of Three-end Block Weave

When considering how to increase the design possibilities of three-end block weave, it might be thought that the use of pick-up was superseded by the far quicker shaft-switching. But pick-up does have definite advantages.

1. It can be started at any moment without any preliminary additions to the loom.
2. It can easily be introduced in just a few places in a design otherwise controlled by the shafts.
3. It can be easily extended to the use of three weft colours.
4. There are certain effects which add no extra time to this already slow technique, but which would be tedious with shaft-switching.
5. Perhaps most importantly, it serves as a very good theoretical introduction to shaft-switching, because the pick-up stick performs so visibly operations which are a little difficult to see and grasp when done by shaft-switching.

In essence, both techniques are doing the same thing – they are forcing shafts 3 and 4 to relinquish their job of deciding where the blocks are to be and handing over that decision to the weaver. Till now the positioning of blocks has been totally decided by where the threading units of (2,3,1) and of (2,4,1) have been disposed across the warp. Many techniques have been described which try and soften that tyranny by bringing variety into the blocks; but it is only with pick-up and shaft-switching that the weaver is set free and can control his or her own block design *while* weaving.

Of the two methods for pick-up, the Raised End technique will now be described in detail.

Raised end technique

This description assumes the technique is to be worked on a narrow warp already threaded with only nine blocks, i.e. with some areas threaded (2,3,1) and some areas threaded (2,4,1).

Lift 34. However the blocks are threaded, this will raise every third end all across the warp, one from each block; as there are nine blocks there will be nine raised ends, as in *Fig. 69(a)*. Take a rod or narrow stick and thread it through this sheet of warp ends, going over and under ends in any desired manner. See stick 1 in *Fig. 69(a)* which goes under three, over three, under three ends. Remember that wherever the pick-up sticks lies above the ends (shaded part) the following pick of weft will show on the surface of the rug; and wherever it lies below the ends the pick will show on the back. So visible stick = visible pick is the rule which governs the path chosen through the raised ends.

Lower 34, leaving the stick in place.

Lift 1. The rising shed will lift the stick and with it all the ends on shafts 3 and 4 it passed under. The shed will be smaller than usual,

but is largest under the pick-up stick when it is pressed against the reed. Pass weft A in this shed.

Lower 1, leaving the stick in place, so beating is impossible.

Lift 34. Using the first pick-up stick as a guide, thread another stick through the raised ends, but taking an exact opposite course, passing over them where the first stick passed under and vice versa; see upper stick 2, in *Fig. 69(b)*. This manoeuvre for brevity will in future be called pick-down, i.e. the opposite of the pick-up. Remove the first stick leaving the second stick in position, as in *Fig. 69(c)*.

Lower 34,

Lift 1. Again the pick-up stick will be lifted by the rising shed, but this time it will carry up all the ends on shafts 3 and 4 *not* carried up before. Pass weft B in this shed.

Lower 1. Now the stick can be removed and these two picks beaten together.

The above sequence is then repeated exactly, but lifting shaft 2, instead of 1; making a complete repeat of four picks.

The repeat can therefore be abbreviated thus:

Lift 34, pick-up, lower 34, lift 1, weft A, lower 1.
Lift 34, pick-down, lower 34, lift 1, weft B, lower 1. Beat.
Lift 34, pick-up, lower 34, lift 2, weft A, lower 2.
Lift 34, pick-down, lower 34, lift 2, weft B, lower 2. Beat.

To shorten such instructions further, they can be reduced to a diagram, as *Fig. 70*, which by means of the dashes shows that the central three raised ends are the ones involved in the pick-up and pick-down, both when weaving with shaft 1 raised and with 2 raised.

If the above was continued with the stick always taking the same route through the raised ends, a block design would result exactly like a threaded design; see *Fig. 69(d)*. But the beauty of the technique is that at every pick-up stage the first stick can take a different route through the ends (followed of course by an exactly opposite pick-down), thus making the design possibilities unlimited. In fact, if desired, the design could be changed every two picks. But however often it is changed, the first stick is always the leader, the decider of the pattern, the second stick blindly following, taking the opposite course.

Notes
— *The most common mistake is to lift shafts 1 and 2 alternately, instead of 1 twice and then 2 twice; see above. If in any doubt which is the correct shaft to raise, it is always the one which makes the weft catch at the selvage.*
— *The theory behind this is that the stick, as it selects a path through the raised ends, is deciding which of them are to be up, which down for the following weft. So it is, as it were, deciding which part of the warp should behave as if threaded (2,3,1), and which as if threaded (2,4,1).*

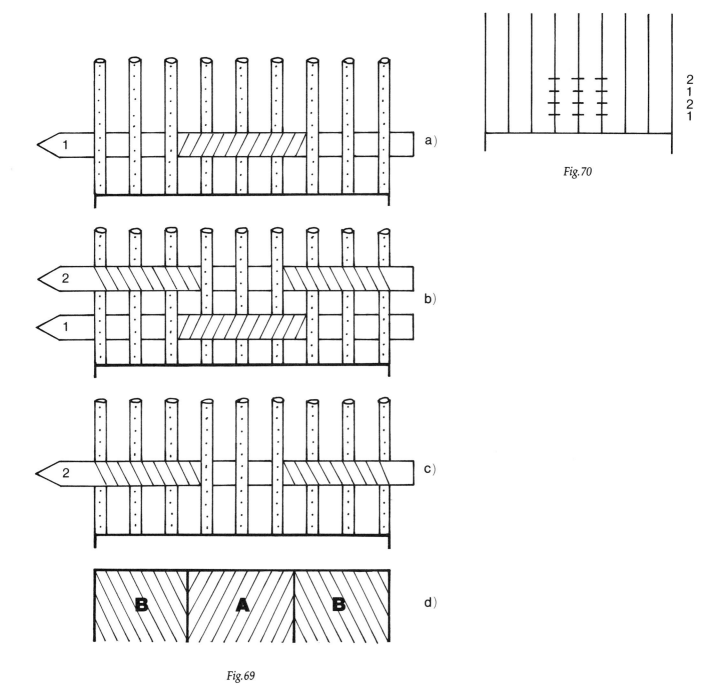

a)

b)

c)

d)

Fig.69

Fig.70

An alternative quicker sequence

It is naturally the picking up and down which slows up the process. By using a slightly different sequence, these manoeuvres can be halved in number.

Lift 34, pick-up, lower 34.

Lift 1, pass weft A, lower 1.

Lift 2, pass weft A, lower 2, so the pick-up stick stays in position for these two picks.

Lift 34, pick-down, lower 34.

Lift 2, pass weft B, lower 2.

Lift 1, pass weft B, so again the stick stays in position for two picks. Lower 1.

With this sequence, all four picks can be beaten together, giving a better chance for the wefts to slide in front of or behind each other. The design can be changed after the first pick of A or of B; so the stick will have to be altered to a new pick-up or pick-down position and not left in place as described above.

Plate 47 (see p. 88)

Plate 48 (see p. 96)

Producing striped and spotted areas

If the pick-up position is changed markedly after every two picks (one of weft A, one of B), areas of vertical stripes as well as of solid colour can be woven. In *Fig. 71(a)*, the position for the pick-up (and of course the pick-down) involves the central five raised ends when weaving on 1, but extends three ends either side (involving the central 11) when weaving on 2. Repeating this alternation of two pick-up positions gives a central area of solid colour with vertical stripes on either side, as shown immediately below. So areas of vertical stripes become a third design element and can be placed at will; see *Fig. 71(b)* and *(c)*. see central diamond in plate 51 (p. 99).

In a similar way, areas of cross-stripes and of spots can be woven, as shown in *Fig. 72(a)* and *(b)*. See Plate 48 (p. 95).

These techniques greatly increase the design possibilities.

Producing oblique stripes

If a piece of this woven block weave is folded obliquely, a natural twill line is seen because the structure is almost a 2/1 twill. By following this natural diagonal line exactly, a very convincing oblique join between two colours can be made. But the junction will look straight and clean only on one side of the rug, the upper as woven; on the back it has an irregular stepped character. It is impossible to make a clean junction on both sides, as it would be with tapestry technique.

The rules involved can be illustrated in the weaving of an oblique stripe three pick-up threads wide; see *Fig. 73*. The problem is knowing when in the cycle to change the pick-up position. Now, if, as in *Fig. 73(a)*, the stripe is to incline up to the right, then the pick-up position must be shifted over one thread to the right after the two picks (with A and B) with shaft 1 raised. Four picks are then woven in the new position and the position again changed. The arrows at the side mark these change-over positions, and the dashes in the centre are seen to move to the right accordingly.

Though from the pick-up positions in the diagram it looks as if the stripe will move up in definite steps, it will in fact have perfectly straight edges because of the way the threads lie in the woven structure. See Plate 49 (p. 98).

There is thus seen to be a change of pick-up position after every four picks. The same is true for a stripe inclined up to the left, as in *Fig. 73(b)*, except that here the pick-up position is changed after weaving with shaft 2 raised; see the arrows.

Following these rules gives clean edges to the stripe on the front of the rug, stepped edges on the back; compare Plates 49 and 50 (p. 98) showing the front and back of a sample respectively. Disobeying the rules means the stepped edge will be on the front, the clean at the back. Of course, both types can be combined on one side of a rug.

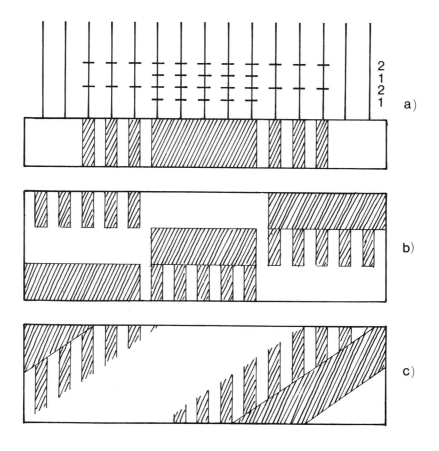

Fig.71

— This clean edge can only lie at one angle, because the pick-up position has to change every four picks. The angle can be altered only by varying the warp setting or the weft thickness, in other words, the epi or the ppi. If the pick-up position were changed after 6, 8 or 10 picks, the stripe would be much steeper but would have a definitely stepped outline, on both the back and the front of the rug.

— A stripe only one pick-up thread wide gives disconnected spots on the back of the rug.

Fig. 74 shows how to change the pick-up positions when weaving a zigzag.

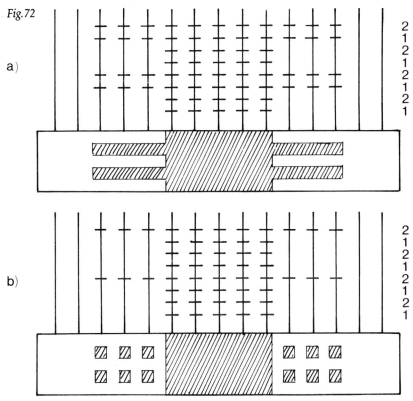

Fig.72

a)

b)

Fig.73

a)

b)

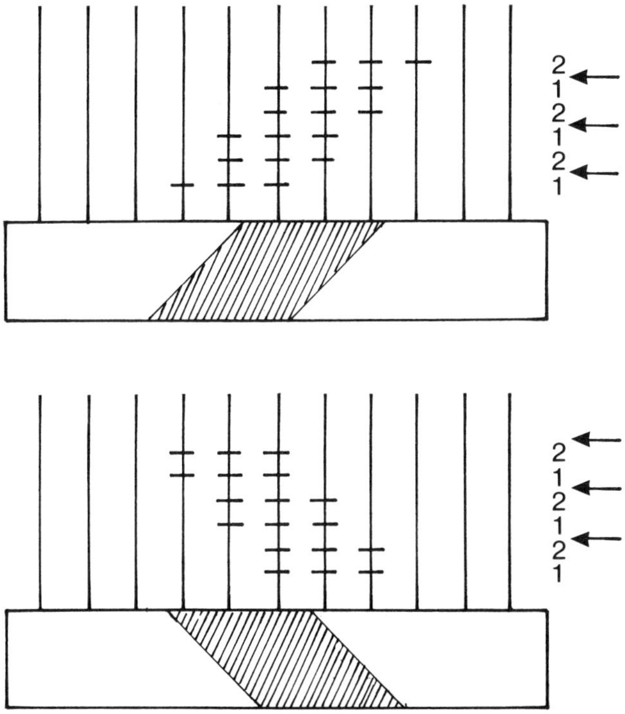

Fig.74

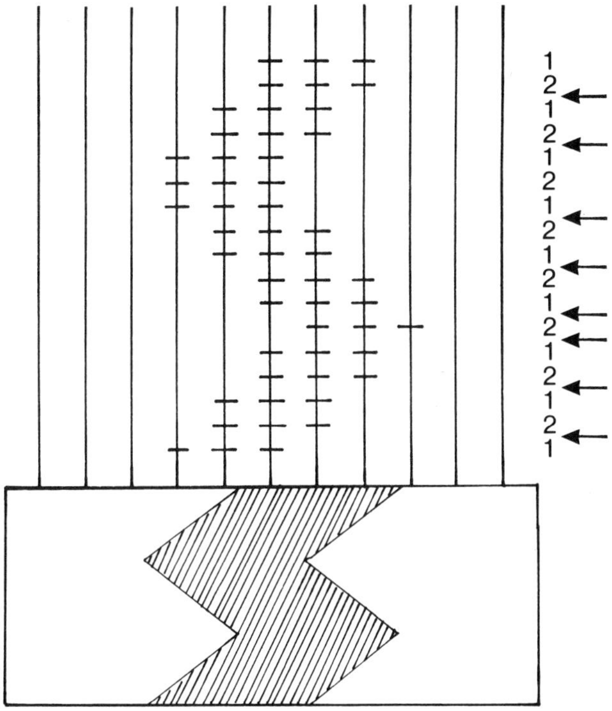

Plate 49 (see p. 96)

Plate 50 (see p. 96)

BACK

Plate 51 (see p. 100)

Weaving a diamond

As might be expected a diamond with its two oblique edges needs a change of pick-up position every two picks.

Start by picking up a single raised end, but make sure you do so when the following two wefts will weave with shaft 1 raised; see *Fig. 75*. These picks establish the point of the diamond. The next stage is to pick up the first end plus the one to its *right* (see diagram) and weave with shaft 2 raised. Then add one end to the *left* (making three being picked up in all) and weave with shaft 1 raised.

Continue in this way, adding one end to the pick-up position, alternately to right and to left, after every two picks. To help keep track, notice that when weaving with shaft 2 raised (an even number), an even number of ends are picked up; when weaving with shaft 1 (an odd number), an odd number are picked up.

When a diamond has reached its full width, decrease its size by reversing the procedure exactly, i.e. the last end added to the pick-up position is the first one to be dropped.

When weaving a shape like this, it is always best to insert the motif's weft first, then the background weft. Mistakes are more quickly seen and rectified. Plate 51 (p. 99) shows a sample based on diamond shapes.

Note
— No arrows are drawn in Fig. 75 *because there is a change of pick-up position after* every *two picks.*

Partial pick-up

This variation allows the blocks produced by the threading to be altered as much as desired by means of pick-up. Let *Fig. 76(a)* represent the blocks resulting from the threading and *(b)* how they are to be altered. The work is done as follows:

Weave the blocks normally, lifting (13,14,23,24) until the point in the design where the openings begin.

Then lift 4. These ends will be raised in three groups corresponding to the three blocks; see *Fig. 76(c)*. Pick-up, passing the stick *under* the ends where the openings are wanted; see stick 1 in diagram.

Lower 4.
Lift 13, pass weft A, the colour forming the blocks. Lower 13.
Lift 4, pick-down; see stick 2 in diagram. Remove first stick.
Lower 4.
Lift 1, pass weft B, the background colour. Remove stick and beat.
The second half of the sequence can be abbreviated thus:
Lift 4, pick-up as before. Lower 4.
Lift 23, weft A. Lower 23.
Lift 4, pick-down as before. Lower 4.
Lift 2, weft B. Remove stick, beat.

Note
— The ends of a block which is not being altered, e.g. the narrow central block in Fig. 76, *are passed over by the first stick and passed under by the second.*

The single block at the centre of Plate 52 (p. 102) has been treated in this way.

In a similar way, the blocks threaded on (2,3,1), i.e. the background areas in *Fig. 76*, can be selectively altered; *Fig. 76(d)* shows a possible result. The sequence in summarized form is as follows:

Lift 3, pick-up, passing the stick over the ends which are to be altered. Lower 3.
Lift 1, weft A. Lower 1.
Lift 3, pick-down. Lower 3.
Lift 14, weft B. Lower 14.
Lift 3, pick-up. Lower 3.
Lift 2, weft A. Lower 2.
Lift 3, pick-down. Lower 3.
Lift 24, weft B. Lower 24. Beat.

Three-colour pick-up

In the normal structure of this block weave, a weft which shows on the front of the rug slides down and almost completely obscures the corresponding weft on the back. Using three colours, the one visible on the front endeavours to hide the other two which lie together in the same shed at the back. So it has an unbalanced structure, and though the front can with care give the appearance of a solid colour, the back will always show a mixture of two colours. The method is worked as follows:

Lift 34, insert a pick-up stick in some fashion; see the lower stick, 1, in *Fig. 77*. Lower 34.
Lift 1, pass weft A which will show where the stick went over the raised ends. Lower 1.
Lift 34, insert second stick. This is *not* a pick-down, i.e. the opposite of the previous pick-up. It is just another pick-up passing over more of the raised ends. It could be inserted as stick 2 in the diagram. Lower 34. Remove stick 1.
Lift 1, pass weft B. Lower 1.
Lift 34, insert the third stick so that the ends not passed over previously are now covered; see stick 3 in *Fig. 77*. Lower 34. Remove stick 2.
Lift 1, pass weft C. Remove stick 3 and beat all three wefts together.

Repeat the above procedure exactly but lifting shaft 2, instead of 1, for the next three insertions of A, B, and C. Continue in this way, three picks with 1 raised, followed by three picks with 2 raised. The bottom of *Fig. 77* shows how the resulting blocks relate exactly to the three pick-ups made.

Note
— *Despite what* Fig. 77 *shows, there is never any moment when all three pick-up sticks are together in the warp.*

It will be understood that the picking-up is more difficult than with only two colours. The only rule is that the three pick-ups *considered together* must cover all the raised ends. The three-colour blocks produced can naturally be moved, have angled junctions and so on, just as in the two-colour version. See Plate 53 (p. 103) where the three colours have been arranged differently in each repeat of the diamond.

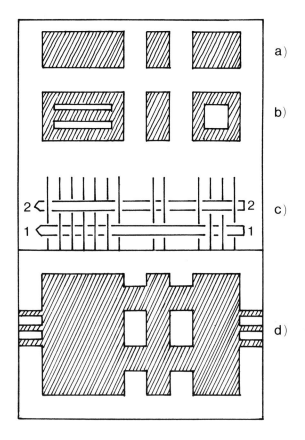

Fig.76

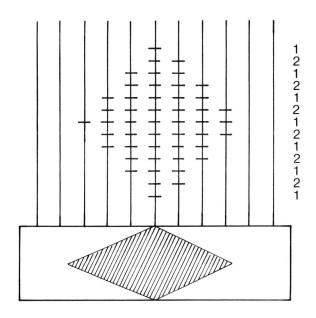

Fig.75

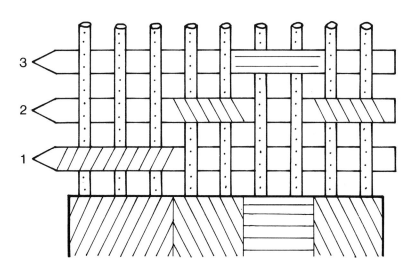

Fig.77

Plate 52 (see p. 100)

Plate 53 (see p. 101)

Plate 53 (see p. 101)

Shaft-switching Applied to Three-end Block Weave

In the search for greater freedom in the placing and movement of blocks, a weaver naturally thinks of using more shafts. Indeed, the three-end block weave can be extended in this way – each new shaft added giving one more controllable block. *Fig. 78 (a)* shows one possibility using six shafts and, below, the sort of design which could be woven. At the right are the sixteen different lifts. It is just possible, using both feet with the pedal tie-up shown at (*b*), to produce all the lifts required by this six-shaft version. But this is about the limit; if a design demands more than six shafts, then a mechanism like a dobby or Jacquard is needed to control them.

It was this realization that led me to another approach. If the four-shaft version is examined – *Fig. 79(a)* – it can be seen that the only difference between the two threading units used is the warp ends on shafts 3 and 4. The ends on shafts 1 and 2 occur regularly right across the warp; they are just the tie-down ends and cannot be involved in controlling the blocks. But it is *because* there is a warp end on shaft 3 in the (2,3,1) blocks that colour B appears on the surface; and *because* there is a warp end on shaft 4 in the (2,4,1) blocks that colour A appears on the surface. The ends on shafts 3 and 4 are, in other words, the *pattern-controlling* ends.

So if it were possible to switch ends from shaft 3 to 4, and back again, *while weaving*, the boundaries between blocks could be moved at will. The blocks would no longer need to be rectangles whose placing is rigidly controlled by the initial threading of the warp, and any two-colour design could be woven with ease. For example, if a warp end on shaft 3 was somehow moved on to shaft 4 (see right-hand arrow), that block changes from a (2,3,1) to a (2,4,1) block, making the design alter from that at (*b*) to that at (*c*). If then an end on shaft 4 was moved to shaft 3 (see left-hand arrow), that block is changed to (2,3,1) and the design now becomes that shown at (*d*).

This is the theory behind shaft-switching, a method which combines the speed of normal block weaving with the freedom of design formerly possible only with pick-up. Taken to its logical conclusion, it can be applied to every threading unit in the width of a rug, say, fifty in all. The loom, though possessing only four shafts and using only four pedals, would have the designing potential of a fifty-two-shaft loom.

Practical ways of switching ends between two shafts have brought out the inherent ingenuity in weavers. They all assume that ends on shafts 1 and 2 are threaded normally; they concentrate on the manipulation of the pattern-controlling ends, the ones usually threaded on shafts 3 and 4.

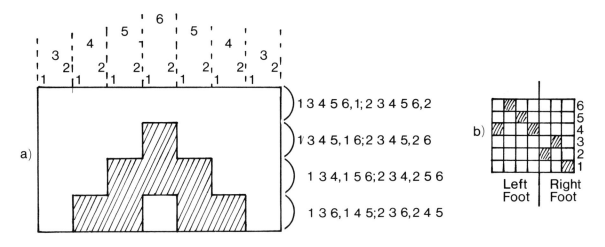

1 3 4 5 6,1; 2 3 4 5 6,2

1 3 4 5,1 6; 2 3 4 5,2 6

1 3 4,1 5 6; 2 3 4,2 5 6

1 3 6,1 4 5; 2 3 6,2 4 5

Fig.78

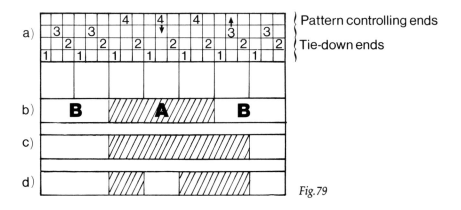

Pattern controlling ends

Tie-down ends

Fig.79

Methods of shaft-switching with pattern-controlling end threaded

(a) REPAIR HEDDLE

A simple solution is to thread the relevant end on a metal repair heddle which is clipped to either shaft 3 or 4 as required; see *Fig. 80(a)*.

(b) FREE HEDDLE

In a similar method the end is threaded on a string heddle which has a small weight at the bottom and a loop at the top. Pins are driven either directly into the tops of shafts 3 and 4, or into removable wood strips which can be fixed to these shafts. The loop on the heddle is then hooked over a pin on shaft 3 or 4; see *Fig. 80(b)*.

(c) METAL HOOK

A stiff wire is bent so there is an eye in the middle and a hook at its upper end; see *Fig. 80(c)*. The warp end is passed through the eye and the wire can be twisted so the hook engages with either shaft 3 or 4.

Methods (b) and (c) work only with a rising-shed loom, as there is nothing to draw the end down positively if the shaft to which it is attached is lowered.

Methods of shaft-switching with pattern-controlling end unthreaded

All these methods depend on having an empty heddle on shafts 3 and 4 between which, or beside which, the warp end passes; see *Fig. 81*. They differ in the way the end is attached to either one or other of the empty heddles.

Fig.80

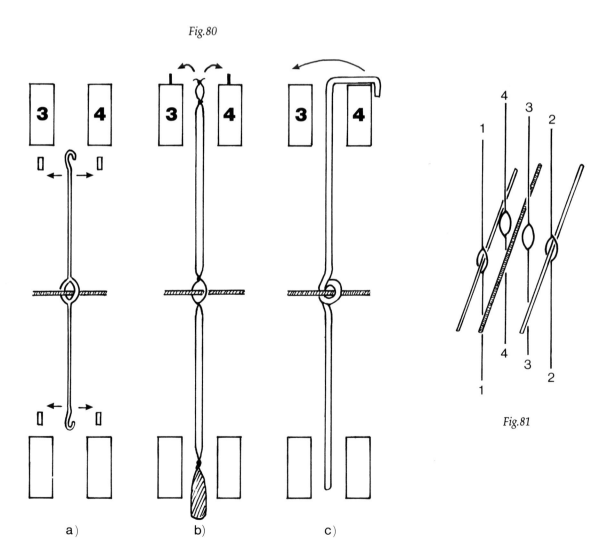

a)   b)   c)

Fig.81

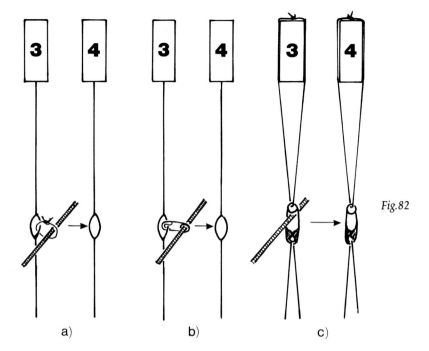

Fig.82

a)   b)   c)

(a) PATTERN-CONTROLLING END
ATTACHED DIRECTLY TO THE HEDDLE EYE

1. Probably the simplest method of all (and the one I first
tried) is to tie the warp end to the eye of one of the empty
heddles with a short length of strong yarn, perhaps the same
as the warp material; see *Fig. 82(a)*. To switch shafts this
loop is either untied or cut and the end tied to the eye of the
other heddle. This is a useful way of setting up a block
weave on a sample warp when teaching. The ties can remain
unaltered while the normal block weaves are explored; then
cut and perhaps replaced with method (b)(1), below, when
shaft-switching is reached.
2. A little more sophisticated than the above is the use of
some sort of snap hook; see *Fig. 82(b)*. This is threaded on
the warp end and can be clipped into the empty eye of either
heddle. A size 12 or 14 snap swivel (used by fishermen),
with the swivel end cut off, is said to work well, though it is
very stiff to open. A small safety pin is another possibility.
The larger the hook or pin, the more the depth of the shed
will be reduced.
3. Another approach is to make special heddles of which the
eyes are actually snap hooks or safety pins, the rest being
heddle twine; see *Fig. 82(c)*.

These methods all work with a rising and falling shed, but
shaft-switching at warp level is not easy; and with a complex
design there can be no numbering system to help the weaver.

(b) PATTERN-CONTROLLING END
ATTACHED INDIRECTLY TO HEDDLE EYE

All these methods depend on the introduction of two loops

or doups; see *Fig. 83(a)*. One loop goes around the warp
end, through the empty eye of the heddle on shaft 3 and then
upwards; the other loop takes a similar course in relation to
the heddle on shaft 4. Now if some way is found of tightening
the loop on 3, the warp end will be pulled over to the empty
heddle eye. It will lie close beside it, not through it; but
whenever shaft 3 is moved, that warp end will behave *as if* it
were threaded on shaft 3. Similarly, if this loop were now
loosened and the loop on 4 tightened, the same warp end
will be pulled over to the empty heddle eye on shaft 4 and
will behave *as if* threaded on 4.

The methods now described differ only in the ways the
two loops are loosened and tightened; they share the great
advantage that the shaft-switching is controlled, not at warp
level, but at the top of the shafts which is far more convenient
for the weaver.

1. Two Loops and Two Constrictor Knots

The two loops are arranged exactly as in *Fig. 83(a)*, with their
knots at the top and with half of each loop passing in front,
half behind, the relevant shaft. A constrictor knot is tied
around each loop above the shaft; labelled A and B in
diagram. If the loop on shaft 3 is pulled upwards to tighten it,
and its constrictor knot (A) is then slid down until it will go
no further, the warp end will rise and fall with shaft 3; see
Fig. 84(a).

Note
— *The other constrictor knot, B, must be slid to the end of its loop to
give enough slack for this to happen.*

If knot A is now slid up out of the way and knot B slid down,

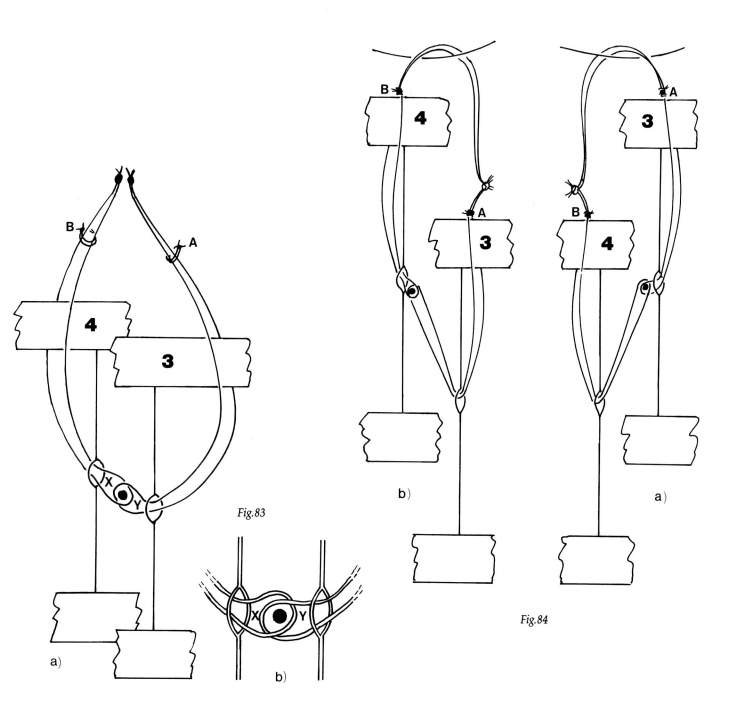

Fig.83

Fig.84

the warp end will rise and fall with shaft 4; see *Fig. 84(b)*.

This method is now described in detail as it is the one most frequently used in workshops and so is the one that introduces many weavers to the idea of shaft-switching.

Practical Details

(a) The Loops

The loops should be made from tightly twisted or cabled yarn, like cotton heddle twine. The yarn has to be strong but not slippery or the constrictor knots will fail to grip.

In length it should be about twice the distance from heddle eye to top of the shaft. A too short loop will impede the

shed; a too long loop will work perfectly but look untidy and get in the way.

At warp level the two loops can be linked together as shown in detail in *Fig. 83(b)*. This is not essential but it means that, when a warp is finished, the loops will be fixed in place ready for the next warp; they cannot slip out of the heddle eyes. When threading such linked loops be sure the warp end goes through both loops and not through the spaces labelled X and Y in *Fig. 83(a)* and *(b)*.

To keep the loops in identifiable pairs, join their upper ends in one knot, as in *Fig. 84(a)* and *(b)*.

To stop the loops tangling or falling down between the shafts, pass them over a cord or rod or some part of the loom above the shafts; see the cord at top of *Fig. 84(a)* and *(b)*. A raddle hung in this position works well and keeps the loops in perfect order. Adjust the height of whatever is used so that the loops can easily slide over it when a shed is opened.

(b) Heddle eyes

There is naturally much friction between the loops and the heddle eyes, so the latter should be as smooth as possible. Twisted wire heddles work well, especially if the eyes are painted with resin or thick enamel to increase their smoothness. The punched-out flat metal heddles will soon fray the loops. If string heddles are used it is important that the shaft is a four-sided rigid frame, not just a top and bottom bar. The latter type can easily be made rigid with vertical wooden strips joining the ends of the two bars.

(c) Constrictor knot

The character of this knot is vital. As *Fig. 84(a)* shows, it is only the fact that knot A is gripping the loop securely that ensures the warp end is lifted with shaft 3. Any slippage here would lead to a progressively smaller shed. The knot must also be loose enough to slide up and down the loop to make the shaft-switching possible.

A good material to use is a harsh wool, like carpet wool, perhaps two- or three-fold; the best knot is a constrictor knot, tied as follows:

Holding the two ends, make a loop between the hands, the part from the left hand crossing over the part from the right, as shown in *Fig. 85(a)*. Put the left index *up* into the loop and the right index *down* into the loop. Twist the right hand away from you, until the two index fingers can touch. Slip the loop from the left index on to the right index. The finished knot is now on the right index and can be transferred on to the shaft-switching loop. Tighten by pulling on the two free ends until it is difficult to slide the knot up and down the loop, see arrows in *Fig. 85(b)*.

Before even making the shaft-switching loops, ensure by experiment that the materials available for them and the knots will work together satisfactorily. The whole system will fail or need constant adjustment if the knots slip when they should be holding.

It is helpful to colour-code the knots. If the colours are, say, red for the shaft 3 loops and blue for the shaft 4 loops, then on every pair of loops either the red or blue must be *down*, tight against the top of the shaft, and the other *up*. If both red and blue are *up*, the relevant warp thread will not move when a shed is opened; if both red and blue are *down*, something will break or shafts 3 and 4 will act as if stuck together.

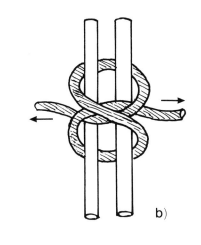

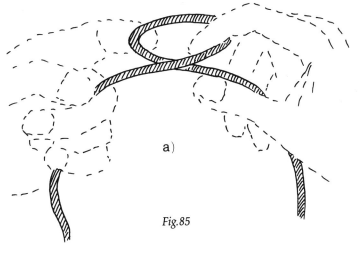

Fig.85

(d) Inverting the threading

It is of course logical to invert the threading so that the tie-down shafts are the two back ones, and the pattern shafts the two front ones, thus making the shaft-switching manipulations conveniently close to the weaver. To avoid having to transpose all the lifts, number the shafts from back to front while threading and tying pedals.

This applies to almost all shaft-switching methods; but the old form of the threading has been maintained here both to avoid confusion and because the two nearest shafts are traditionally used for the tie-down ends.

(e) Recording threadings

Some convention is needed for recording a threading involving shaft-switching. It is here suggested that the two shafts between which the switching is to take place are written one above the other in the same vertical column. The threading now becomes that shown in *Fig. 86(a)*. This can be emphasized by arrows, as in *(b)*, or a circle as in *(c)*. Perhaps the best way is an oblique line, as in *(d)*, as it shows the actual path taken by the warp end between the empty heddles on shafts 3 and 4. This can be written in text as (2,4/3,1).

2. One Loop and One Constrictor Knot.

A natural development from the above method is to make the two loops from one continuous cord. This is a little more difficult to install, but it means that only one constrictor knot is needed; A in *Fig. 87*.

Start with a length four times the height of a heddle.
    If the two ends of the loop are to be linked, as in the diagram, begin with the cord at X and follow the course indicated by arrows, ending at Y, where the two ends are tied together.

If the two ends are not to be linked, the loop can be more simply made in another way; see *Fig. 88*. Tie the cord in a loop around the tops of shafts 3 and 4; see *(a)*. Pull the bottom of the loop upwards; see *(b)*. Pull down the two loops thus made and thread them through the empty heddles, securing them immediately by passing the warp end through both; see *(c)*.

Note
— *In both methods, note the position of the knot joining the two ends of the cord. It must be below the level of the top of the shafts so it will not impede the movement of the single constrictor knot.*

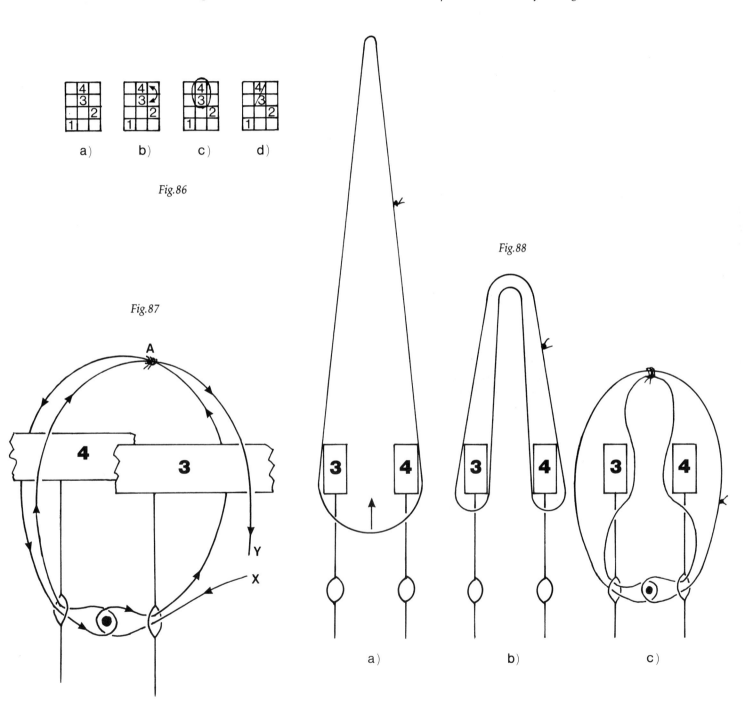

a)   b)   c)   d)

Fig.86

Fig.87

Fig.88

a)   b)   c)

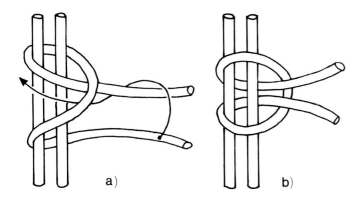

Fig.89

The constrictor knot has to be tied differently as there is no free end to slip it over, as in method 1. *Fig. 89(a)* shows how it is tied around the two elements of the loop above the shafts; see A in *Fig. 88(c)*. *Fig. 89(b)* is an alternative knot, a lark's head, which should then be secured with a square (reef) knot.

The single constrictor knot is either slid down against the top of shaft 3 to make the warp end weave with 3, or against the top of shaft 4 to make it weave with 4. So it is a foolproof method, making it impossible to tighten on both shafts at the same time, as can happen with method 1.

3. Two Loops and Two Boards with Pins

The two-loop method can be refined by replacing the constrictor knots by boards with pins on to which the loops can be hooked to tighten them; see *Figs. 90* and *91*.

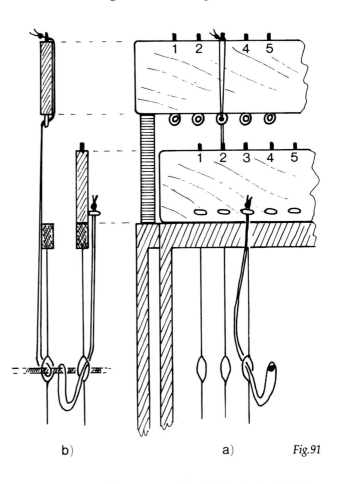

Fig.91

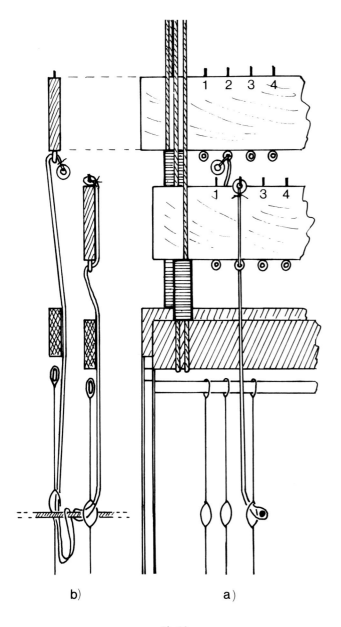

Fig.90

Above each of the shafts concerned, fit a thin board about 4 inches (10 cm) wide and as long as the shafts. For convenience the one further from the weaver should be at least 4 inches (10 cm) higher than the nearer one. With a countermarch or counterbalanced loom this is easy, as the boards can be attached to the cords suspending the shafts using cardboard tubes of appropriate length as distance pieces; see horizontal hatching in *Fig. 90(a)*. On a jack loom, the front board can be fixed directly to the top of the shaft; the rear board needs some intervening piece, see horizontal hatching in *Fig. 91(a)*.

Along the top edge of each board fix small pins or nails (one every ¾ inch (19 mm) if a warp setting of 4 epi is being used), and along the underside small screw-eyes, similarly spaced. The front board on a jack loom has no available underside, so fix the screw-eyes near its lower edge; see *Fig. 91(a)*.

Tie a loop. Pass it down through a screw-eye and then through an empty eye of a heddle. Pass a warp end through to secure it. The upper knotted end of the loop can, for easy handling, have a small ring, paperclip or washer on it. Place this over the nail directly above the screw-eye to tighten the loop. To loosen, just take it off; the ring will prevent it falling further than the screw-eye. If linked loops are wanted, they can be made in pairs then threaded upwards from warp level.

This mode of action implies that the loops must be very accurately made in two sizes, measured from heddle eye to top of appropriate board. Unlike the constrictor knot method, there is no easy adjustment once the loops are tied. The absence of these knots and their need to grip the loop means the latter can be made from smooth, strong, synthetic material, like braided nylon fishing line.

For convenience, number the nails on both boards. This will help to avoid mistakes; if the loop is on nail 5 on the front board, then the corresponding loop *must* be off nail 5 on the back board. Numbers are also useful when weaving from a design worked on a squared grid, as each pair of nails controls the design in one threading unit (= one square).

4. One Length of Texsolv and Nails

Texsolv with its smoothness, strength and regular holes seems made for shaft-switching; its great advantage being that *one* length of Texsolv replaces the *two* loops previously needed. It could for instance be used to simplify the last method. Even simpler is the following method:

Measure lengths of Texsolv about twice the height of a heddle.

Mark the central hole. Pass each length through the empty heddle eyes on the two relevant shafts and bring the ends up above the shafts and tie them together, as in *Fig. 92(a)*.

Insert small screw eyes every ¾ inch (19 mm) along the top of both shafts, assuming these are made of wood. Thread the warp end through the marked central hole.

To make this end weave on shaft A, pull the Texsolv up in front of A as far as possible, then fix it by pushing its nearest hole over the screw-eye; see *Fig. 92(b)*. Mark this hole for future use. To switch shafts, take the Texsolv off this screw-eye, pull up the part behind shaft B and fix it over the screw-eye on B, again marking the hole used. A screw-eye is suggested, rather than a nail, because the Texsolv needs to fit firmly.

This is all that is needed; but the system could be refined with screw-eyes on the front of A and back of B through which the Texsolv passes, by numbering the screw-eyes and so on.

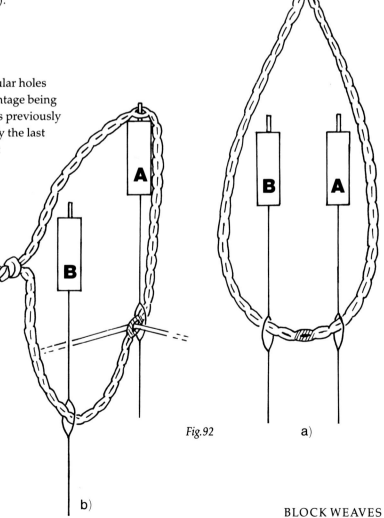

Fig.92 a)

b)

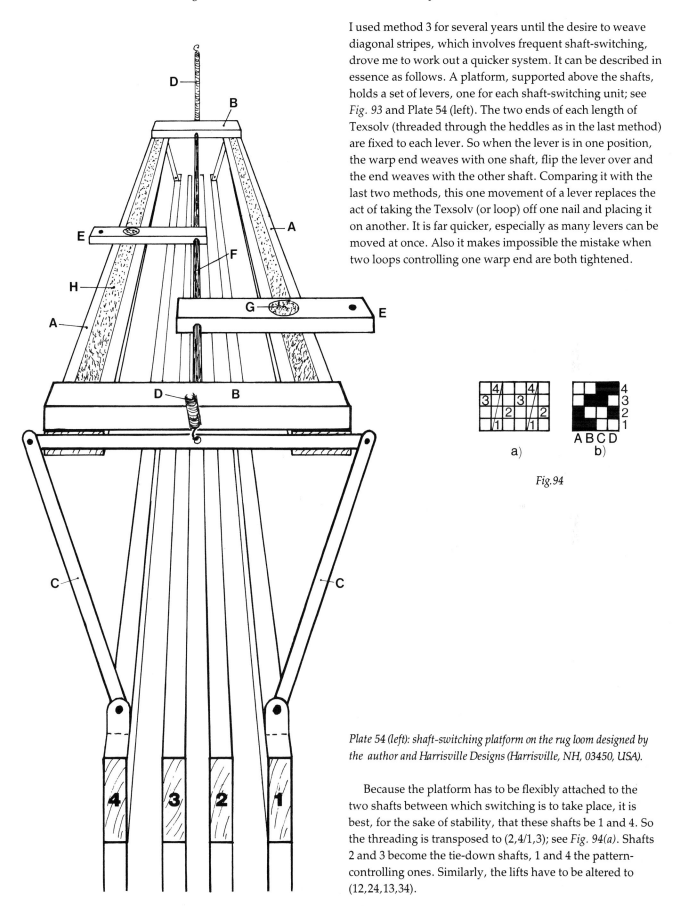

Fig.93

5. Lever System

I used method 3 for several years until the desire to weave diagonal stripes, which involves frequent shaft-switching, drove me to work out a quicker system. It can be described in essence as follows. A platform, supported above the shafts, holds a set of levers, one for each shaft-switching unit; see *Fig. 93* and Plate 54 (left). The two ends of each length of Texsolv (threaded through the heddles as in the last method) are fixed to each lever. So when the lever is in one position, the warp end weaves with one shaft, flip the lever over and the end weaves with the other shaft. Comparing it with the last two methods, this one movement of a lever replaces the act of taking the Texsolv (or loop) off one nail and placing it on another. It is far quicker, especially as many levers can be moved at once. Also it makes impossible the mistake when two loops controlling one warp end are both tightened.

Fig.94

a)   b)

Because the platform has to be flexibly attached to the two shafts between which switching is to take place, it is best, for the sake of stability, that these shafts be 1 and 4. So the threading is transposed to (2,4/1,3); see *Fig. 94(a)*. Shafts 2 and 3 become the tie-down shafts, 1 and 4 the pattern-controlling ones. Similarly, the lifts have to be altered to (12,24,13,34).

The basic structure of the rectangular platform is two lengths of wood, A (slightly shorter than the shafts), joined at their ends by two short cross pieces, B; see perspective view *Fig. 93* and cross-sectional views *Figs. 95* and *96*. The platform is held in position by pivotted metal struts, C, running from the corners of the platform down to the ends of shafts 1 and 4; the pivots allow it to tilt as different shafts are operated. Two springs, D, stretching from the cross pieces at each end to the loom super-structure, help keep the platform in place.

The wooden levers, E, each about ¾ inch (19 mm) wide, are all threaded side by side on one long central rod, F, whose ends are fixed into the cross pieces. At intervals this rod is supported by small metal brackets (not shown) which also give stability to the long pieces of the platform. Each lever has a hole about 3¼ inches (8.25 cm) from the rod, for the two ends of the Texsolv to pass through and be knotted; see *Fig. 95*. These knots provide a way of fine adjusting the Texsolv length. Each lever has a patch of Velcro, G, on either side, placed so that it engages with the long strips of Velcro, H, running the full length of the top of the platform. This simple way of holding the levers in either position replaces the complicated metal springs in my first lever system.

Narrow rods, J, attached to the front and back edge of the platform reduce friction on the Texsolv as it runs down to the heddles, first passing through screw-eyes, K, on the front of shaft 1 or the back of shaft 4; see *Fig. 95*.

The rods, L, going right across the loom keep the shafts from bunching together and rubbing each other, due to the tension in the Texsolv lengths.

Fig.95

Fig.96

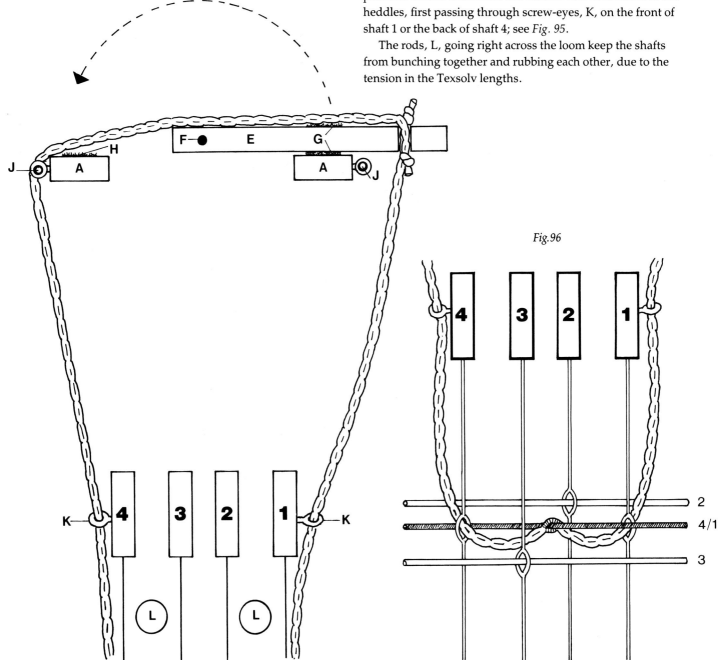

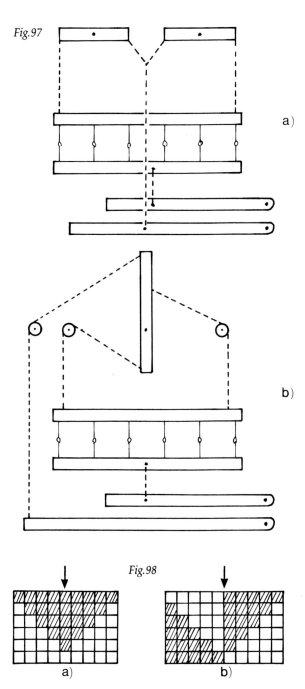

Fig.97

a)

b)

Fig.98

a)   b)

(a) Threading

When threading a warp, keep the levers upright so that the marked hole in the Texsolv is halfway between shafts 1 and 4 and easy to locate. The threading unit of three ends is repeated all across the warp, each unit being exactly as shown in *Fig. 96*, where the switchable end is shaded. If the relevant lever were positioned towards the weaver, as in *Fig. 95*, the left side of the Texsolv would be tightened and the warp end would weave as if on shaft 4. If the lever were then flipped away from the weaver (dotted arrow), the right side of the Texsolv would tighten and the end would weave as if on shaft 1.

(b) Tie-up

Fig. 94(b) gives the tie-up. The pedals are used in the sequence A,C,D,B for weaving the heading, and in the sequence A,D,B,C (using alternate feet) for the rug proper. No other lifts are needed. If for instance a solid colour all across the rug is wanted, the levers are flipped so they all face in one direction and the above sequence used; there is no need to use four special lifts as was done in *Fig. 52(b)* on p. 69.

Once this device is installed, a long warp can be beamed and, without any change of threading or tie-up, a succession of completely different rugs can be woven, their design depending entirely on how the levers are manipulated.

Designing with shaft-switching

Designing with shaft-switching can be daunting because so few limitations are placed on the designer. If the rug is to be 36 inches (91 cm) wide, then it will use $36 \div \frac{3}{4} = 48$ ($91 \div 1.9 = 48$) threading units, because the threading units are $\frac{3}{4}$ inch (19 mm) wide. This could be increased to 50 or 51 to allow for the draw-in. So the design can be represented on squared paper by an area fifty squares wide by, say, eighty to a hundred squares long, depending on the proportion wanted. Any design made by filling in squares in this area can be woven.

It is a good idea to start with some very rough thumbnail sketches and then, when one of these has been selected, to transfer it to squared paper. One basic decision is whether the design will need an odd or even number of units. A design with a central diamond will need an odd number; see *Fig. 98(a)*; but if the diamond is two-coloured, as in *Fig. 98(b)*, it will need an even number. In the first case, the design is centred on a unit (arrowed), in the second case on the junction between two units (also arrowed).

Once the design is on squared paper, find out how many

The ends of the levers can be numbered either outwards from the centre or straight across, making it easy to follow a similarly numbered paper design.

The system as described is intended for a countermarch loom. The cords lifting the shafts must be attached just outside the struts supporting the platform. Such a loom with two sets of horizontal jacks has cords passing centrally down between the shafts; see *Fig. 97(a)*. A lever must be omitted at the centre of the platform to allow these cords to pass through. Alternatively, the action can be altered to the type with one set of vertical jacks which has no such central cords; see *Fig. 97(b)*.

An adaptation of the lever system for a jack loom has been developed and described (see article by Sadye Wilson in *Shuttle, Spindle and Dyepot*, Winter 1978).

picks of weft, *when beaten*, build up into ¾ inch (19 mm). This is vital information. The woven squares are by nature ¾ wide (19 mm), so if the design is to be reproduced exactly, the squares when woven must also be ¾ inch (19 mm) high, i.e. measured in the warp direction. If this is not done, the design will appear either compressed or expanded. Depending on the yarn and strength of beating, this ¾ inch (19 mm) woven length may need between sixteen and twenty-two picks. Remember that the shafts can be switched after a full repeat of the four lifts (= four picks), or after a half repeat (= two picks). Sometimes for complete accuracy one square is woven with sixteen picks (= four repeats of the lifts) and the next is woven with eighteen picks (= four and a half repeats), and this alternation maintained. Sometimes four repeats for one square is almost correct; but occasional checking against the total length shows a slight adjustment is necessary, so the next square is woven with three and a half or four and a half repeats.

The total length is marked up the side of the design, every four squares conveniently measuring 3 inches (7.5 cm), every sixteen a foot (30 cm). See *Fig. 99(a)*. The design can be numbered along its lower edge to tally with the numbering of the levers.

To weave a circle, draw one with compasses on squared paper, making sure its circumference coincides with horizontal and vertical lines where possible; see *Fig. 99(a)*. Then fill in squares as near as possible to the drawn line, as shown in lower half of the diagram. Make it absolutely symmetrical; if the circle starts five squares wide, as in the diagram, then the sides must be five squares high. A snag is encountered here because a weft-face rug contracts more in

its width than its length. So the threading unit (i.e. the square) will in reality be a fraction less than ¾ inch (19 mm) wide in the finished rug, and a circle woven as described can begin to look oval. Counteract this by putting in the 6-inch (15-cm) markers at about 5¾-inch (14.6-cm) intervals, or by 'losing', say, ¾ inch when weaving the vertical sides of the circle.

All the above designs were squared off, but though every unit has to be ¾ inch (19 mm) wide, there is no need for it to be woven ¾ inch (19 mm) high. For example, to weave a design based on the smooth diagonal stripes described for the pick-up technique, the shafts *have* to be switched after every four picks. The design can be notated on squared paper, as in *Fig. 99(b)*, but here a square = four picks, not sixteen or so as previously. So it is only a working drawing and bears little resemblance to the woven result.

Very complex-seeming designs can be woven using areas of narrow warp- and weftway stripes, instead of areas of solid colour. These all depend on abandoning the normal colour sequence and using, for instance, (A,B,A,A) × 2, (B,B,B,A) × 2. With careful shaft-switching, the vertical and horizontal lines can be made to meet diagonally; see Plate 55 (pp. 118–19). Naturally, all the variations shown in *Figs. 55* and *62* can be coupled with shaft-switching.

Note
— *There is no way of distinguishing between a two-coloured three-end block weave rug woven using the pick-up method and one woven using the shaft-switching method. The structure is identical in the two cases, only the method of achieving it differs. The woven illustrations for these two techniques are, therefore, more or less*

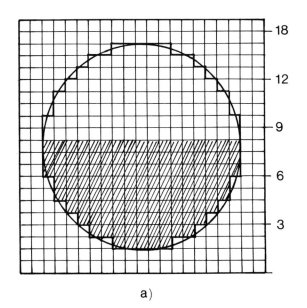

a)

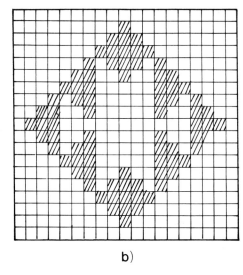

b)

Fig.99

interchangeable. It is when the speed of production is taken into account that the two methods are found to be so different, shaft-switching being incomparably the quicker of the two.

Three-colour version

By using one more shaft, a three-colour block weave controlled by shaft-switching can be woven. *Fig. 100(a)* shows the weave in its threaded form giving three blocks each with one colour on the surface but two at the back. The structure is identical to that obtained with three-colour pick-up.

The shaft-switching version preserves the tie-down ends on shafts 1 and 2, but the pattern ends are arranged so they can be switched between shafts 3, 4 and 5; this gives the threading diagram in *Fig. 100(b)*. Such switching is not possible with the lever system, so one of the simpler methods must be used, such as loops and knots. There has to be a loop passing through an empty heddle on shafts 3, 4 and 5, and the pattern end goes through all three loops; see *Fig. 101*. The constrictor knots must be adjusted so each end weaves with only one of these three shafts at any point in the design. The shafts are lifted as in *Fig. 100* and three wefts, A, B, and C, passed in succession. When shafts 135 are lifted, weft A will appear wherever the ends are weaving with shaft 4, i.e. the pattern shaft *not* lifted. This relationship exists between the other lifts and where the wefts will appear.

If three fairly close colours are chosen, this is a satisfactory weave, but it is not reversible; two colours always lie together in one shed on the back of the rug.

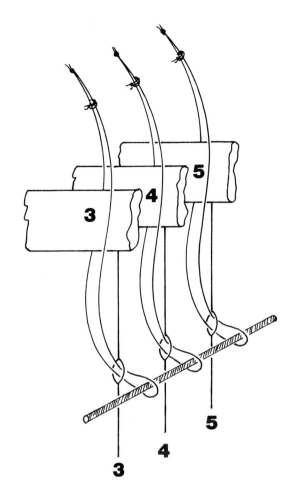

Fig.101

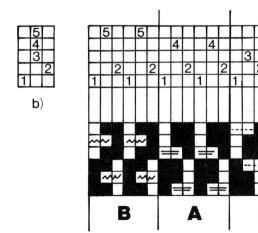

b)

2 4 5	C	----
2 3 4	B	$\sim\!\sim$
2 3 5	A	$=$
1 4 5	C	-----
1 3 4	B	$\sim\!\sim$
1 3 5	A	$=$

a)

Fig.100

Plate 55 (see p. 116)

Applying Shaft-switching to Other Four-shaft Block Weaves

(a) Four-end Block Weave

This block weave, with its threading units of (1,3,2,3) and (1,4,2,4), is often chosen by weavers because it gives areas of solid colour without the colour at the back showing through on the front. By lifting (13,14,23,24) and throwing two colours alternately, blocks are produced in which the weft weaves over 3, under 1 end on both the front and back of the rug; see *Fig. 102(a)*. This long float is often reduced by weaving at a relatively high warp setting. With rag wefts and a high warp setting, the warp is not covered, but the blocks still appear as the back weft slides so well behind the front weft in each pair of picks.

Shaft-switching can be applied to this block weave in two ways.

1. Switching the two pattern ends in a unit together. If both the ends on shaft 3 were switched to 4, as shown by arrows in *Fig. 102(a)*, the weave plan becomes the one in *Fig. 102(b)*. The colour A block will move four threads over to the right, as shown; at 6 epi this means a shift of ⅔ inch (1.7 cm). These two ends can be economically switched if their controlling loops are treated *in pairs*. So depending on the method being used, they could share the same constrictor knot, be placed over the same nail on a board or be connected to the same lever. As details differ in each case, *Fig. 103(a)* gives a general diagram; it shows how two loops going through shaft 3 heddles are joined together and are moved as a unit, and how the same happens to the two loops going through shaft 4 heddles. This threading can be written as in *Fig. 103(b)*; or, if using the lever system, in its transposed form as in *Fig. 103(c)*.

2. Switching pattern ends individually.
Fig. 102(c) shows what happens when only the left hand of the arrowed ends on shaft 3 is switched to 4. The A block moves only two ends (= ⅓ inch [8.5 mm] at 6 epi) to the right, giving much finer adjustment in a design. But of course every pattern end has to be controlled separately, which means twice as many constrictor knots, or levers or nails on a board. The sample in Plate 56 (right) was woven in this way.

However, once these are installed, the possibilities are greatly increased, because not only can the four-end block weave be woven with much finer detail, but the threading also gives everything obtainable from the Double Two-Tie Unit draft.

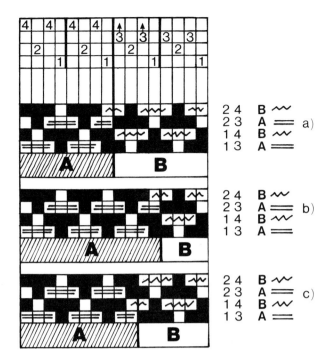

Fig.102

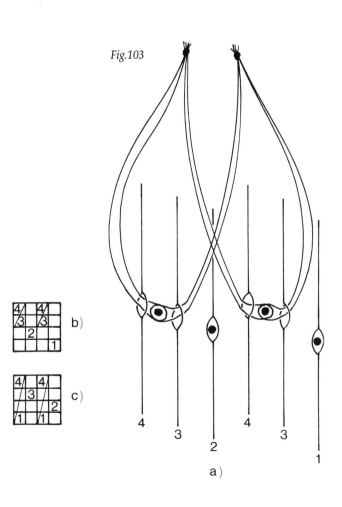

Fig.103

Plate 56 (see left)

Plate 57 (see p. 124)

Plate 58 (see p. 124)

For example, consider this threading if the pattern ends are alternately on shafts 3 and 4, as in *Fig. 104(a)*. Lifting this as shown (the lifts used in the block weave in a different order), gives a 2/2 twill moving up to the left. If now the two central pattern ends are switched (arrows), the twill alters direction below the switched ends; see *Fig. 104(b)*.

This is easier to understand if the twill results from a straight draft, as in *Fig. 104(c)*, for switching the two similarly placed ends produces an obvious reverse in the threading direction, as in *Fig. 104(d)*. This reversal of twill direction by means of shaft-switching means that designs based on the colour sequences suitable for 2/2 twill, such as (A,A,B), can be worked. The result will be controllable areas of oblique stripes in the two directions; see Plate 57 (p. 122) in which the shafts have been switched in sequence to the right after every six picks. Designs become very bold if the twill is woven on opposites with alternating wefts, so that the sequence is (12,34;23,14;34,12;14,23). Plate 58 (p. 123) shows one possibility, in which a single end is switched at each boundary of the diamonds after every four picks. The diamond is outlined in red or white depending on whether the switching starts at the beginning of the lifting sequence or halfway through it. Plate 59 (p. 126) shows that a spiral can be woven by staggering the twill reversal points in the two halves of the diamond. Because of its short floats and frequent use of opposite lifts, this weave works well with a warp of 4 epi and a weft of carpet wool used three-fold.

Taking this a step further, a whole new field opens up if the warp is woven partly as a block weave, i.e. with the shafts switched to give areas of either (1,3,2,3) or (1,4,2,4), and partly as a twill, i.e. with the shafts switched to give (1,3,2,4). It has been noted that the lifts for a twill are those normal for a block weave in a slightly different but usable order, so combining the two structures is feasible. If, therefore, the shafts are lifted as for a twill (straight, broken or on opposites) and an appropriate weft colour sequence used, a small-scale twill pattern will appear in the twill-threaded areas of the warp and some other quite different pattern will appear in the block-threaded areas.

Plate 60 (p. 127) shows this plainly. The weft sequence (A,A,A,B,A,A,B,B,A,B,B,B) was used, the shafts being lifted to give a straight twill (13,23,34,14); this gives the familiar small triangle design. By shaft-switching, this twill area was moved diagonally. The block weave areas show either A spotted with B, if threaded (1,3,2,3), or B spotted with A, if threaded (1,4,2,4).

There is a small technical problem in that the weft in the block weave areas, which passes over three ends, under one, packs down more closely than that in the twill areas, which passes over two, under two. To preserve a straight fell, the design must take this into consideration. One obvious solution is to counter-change areas of twill and block weave. Another is the one shown in Plate 60 (p. 127), where the twill area moves regularly across the rug, so whatever irregularities may occur on the way, the fell is straight when the design is completed. This was woven at 5 working epi and with a weft of 2-ply carpet wool, used three-fold.

(b) Six-end Block Draft

This draft has the advantage that it can be quickly derived from the much-used three-end draft. By rethreading, in reverse order, alternate pairs of ends on shafts 1 and 2, the three-end draft in *Fig. 105(a)* becomes the six-end draft, in *Fig. 105(b)*. The latter gives several block weaves all containing 3-span floats.

1. Using the familiar block weave lifts (13,14,23,24) and an (A,B,A,B) colour sequence.
2. Using 2/2 twill lifts (12,23,34,14) and three wefts in an (A,B,A,C) sequence. Wefts B and C are normal thickness and form floats on back and front. Weft A should be thinner; it shows slightly all across on back and front. It can be the same colour as B or C, or a colour that works with both. When switching shafts, remember the threading unit is six ends and so has two 3s or 4s in it. Therefore two adjacent levers (or four or six) must be moved together.
3. With the pattern ends attached alternately on shafts 3 and 4 for one block, and on shafts 4 and 3 for the other block, as in *Fig. 105(c)*. When woven with the lifts

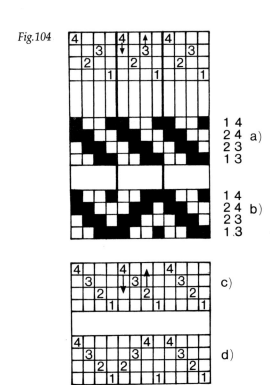

Fig.104

1 4
2 4 a)
2 3
1 3

1 4
2 4 b)
2 3
1 3

c)

d)

(13,23,24,14) and an (A,B,A,B) colour sequence, this gives a block weave in which the colours do not reverse on the back. Each weft weaves over three, under three in one block, and plain in the next block.

4. Repeating the first and third pick of the last weave several times, then the second and fourth several times, gives a structure like the M's and O's weave, which is not very suitable for weft-face rugs.

The most interesting use of this draft is not a block weave at all; it relies on the fact that if the pattern ends are attached alternately to shafts 3 and 4 all across the warp, the threading becomes a pointed four-shaft draft. Plain weave is then possible by lifting 13 and 24; see *Fig. 105(d)*. Now if at any moment a single end is switched from 4 to 3, or vice versa, a 3-span float will appear on the back and front of the rug. In *Fig. 105(e)*, the arrowed end, previously on shaft 4, has been switched to 3 and the weave plan below shows the floats this produces. Such floats naturally weaken the structure, so can be permitted for only a few picks, say, four or six. The relevant end is then switched back to its original shaft and perhaps the next available pattern end to right or left switched; this time it would be from shaft 3 to 4. Continuing like this in a regular way, an oblique ridge of floats can be built up. Plate 61 (pp. 130-1) shows a design based on these ridges; they

are most visible if, as in this example, a light-coloured weft is used. If two colours of weft are employed, then floats of either colour can be placed on a ground of stripes; see Plate 62 (pp. 130–1).

This controlled production of floats, rather than areas of colour, is an unexpected bonus from the shaft-switching system. The warp should have 4 working epi, and the weft should be 2-ply carpet wool used two-or three-fold.

(c) Draft Based on a Straight Three-shaft Draft

This block weave (which I derived from the one called 'Crackle' by Mary Atwater) has great possibilities, as it not only gives blocks of two solid colours, but a third block of warpway stripes of these two colours as well. Moreover, these three blocks can be positioned in many different ways relative to the four threading units. It lends itself well to shaft-switching, which can be carried out between any two adjacent blocks, and was in fact the first block weave to which I applied the system.

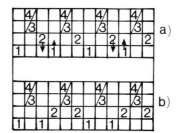

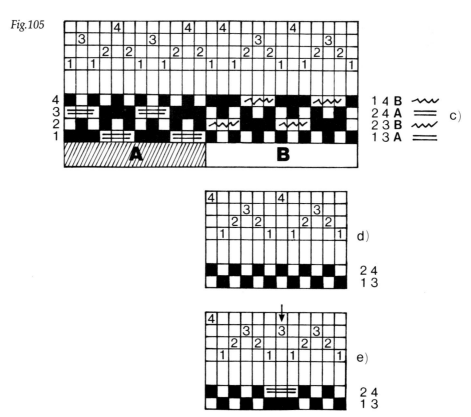

Fig.105

Plate 59 (see p. 124)

Plate 60 (see p. 124)

Fig. 106(a) shows a symmetrical arrangement of three of the available threading units. These are woven with 2/2 twill lifts and with wefts in a (A,A,B,B) colour sequence. The result is a central block of colour B, flanked by blocks striped with A and B, bordered with blocks of colour A; see bottom of diagram. Note that due to the way the colours lie, two of the threading units have to be increased in size to achieve symmetry in the woven blocks.

It will immediately be seen that threading units II and III are those of the three-end block weave. Also that threading unit I can be easily derived from the latter block weave by moving an end from shaft 2 to 3, as shown in *Fig. 107(a)* and *(b)*. So with very little rethreading a loom set up for the three-end block weave can be changed to the present weave and vice versa.

Fig. 106(b) shows the altered threading and it will be understood that, by shaft-switching in the central area, any shape of colour B can be made on a background of stripes; the outer blocks of colour A will remain unchanged; see Plate 63 (p. 132).

Using other colour sequences, areas of solid colour disappear and the design resolves into areas of different types of striping. Plate 64 (p. 133) shows a rug based on a colour sequence of (A,A,B,B) × 4, (B,B,A,A) × 4. Plate 65 (pp. 133) shows one sometimes using (A,B,B,B) × 2, (A,B,A,A) × 2, and sometimes (B,B,B,A) × 2, (A,B,A,A) × 2. All these colour sequences require a floating selvage. The warp has 4 working epi and the weft is 2-ply carpet wool used three-fold.

Three-colour Block Weave

When many two-colour block weaves can be woven on four shafts, it is surprising to realize that, in order to weave a balanced three-colour block weave, twice that number is needed. The problem is how to hide the third colour in the structure of the rug, when the other two are showing on the front and back. The two solutions now described are really developments of the three-end and four-end block weaves.

(a) Three-colour Block Weave Based on the Three-end Draft

Fig. 108(a) shows the threading and weave plan and it will be seen that, as with the three-end draft, shafts 1 and 2 occur regularly across the threading and carry the tie-down warp ends. But instead of there being single pattern ends, they are in pairs on shafts 3 and 4, 5 and 6, and 7 and 8. So in block I the threading is (2,3,4,1), in block II it is (2,5,6,1), and in block III (2,7,8,1).

The structure is best understood from the thread diagrams, *Fig. 108(b)* and *(c)*, which show the first three picks in block I. Here it is seen that the pattern ends 3 and 4 move as a *pair* when wefts A (showing on the back) and C (showing on the front) are inserted. But they *separate* to allow B (the hidden weft at this point) to pass between them. As the cross-section shows, the pair actually lie one above the other and to this end are sleyed through the same dent in the reed. In the remaining three picks of the repeat, the pattern ends move in exactly the same way, but it is shaft 2 which is raised throughout, not 1. The threading units can be arranged in any sequence.

With a three-colour block weave there are many ways the shafts can be lifted – each giving a different arrangement of the three colours (or only two of them) on the front, together with different arrangements on the back. In fact, there are more possibilities than any loom has pedals. The way to approach this problem is to pick a set of lifts which gives a different colour in each of the three blocks and ensures that each colour weaves in the front, centre and back; *Fig. 109(a)*,

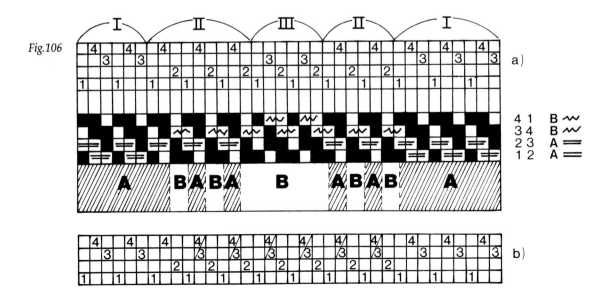

Fig.106

a)

4 1   B 〜
3 4   B 〜
2 3   A ═
1 2   A ═

b)

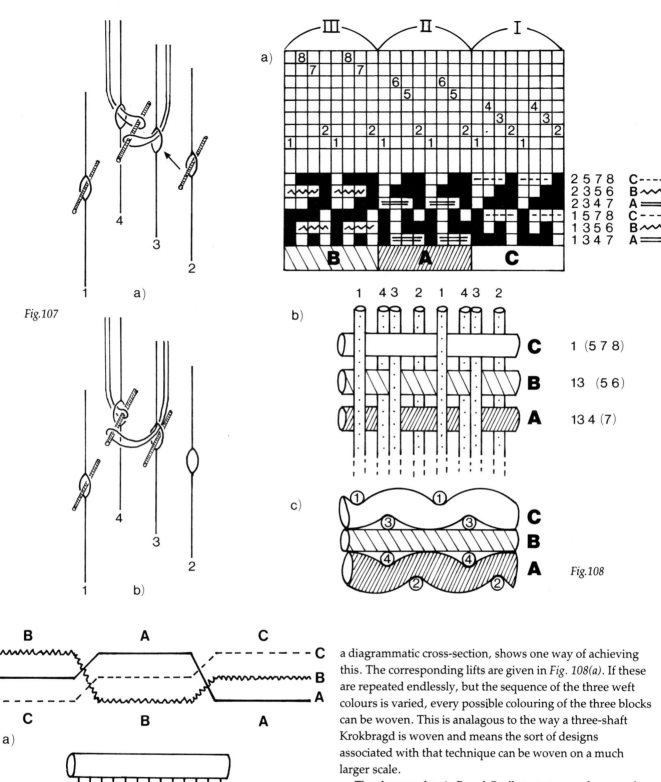

Fig.107

Fig.108

Fig.109

a diagrammatic cross-section, shows one way of achieving this. The corresponding lifts are given in *Fig. 108(a)*. If these are repeated endlessly, but the sequence of the three weft colours is varied, every possible colouring of the three blocks can be woven. This is analagous to the way a three-shaft Krokbragd is woven and means the sort of designs associated with that technique can be woven on a much larger scale.

The three wefts, A, B and C, all start at one selvage and the three picks are beaten in together to encourage good coverage. The colour sequence can then easily be changed to (A,C,B), (B,A,C), (C,B,A) or whatever is wished. If it is changed to, say, (A,A,C), so that two of the blocks show the same colour, simply stop colour B and replace it with a second shuttle of A. In this way, the selvage to selvage passage of three wefts is not interrupted and the edges stay perfect. See Plate 66 (pp. 134–5).

Plate 61 (see p. 125)

Plate 62 (see p. 125)

BLOCK WEAVES **131**

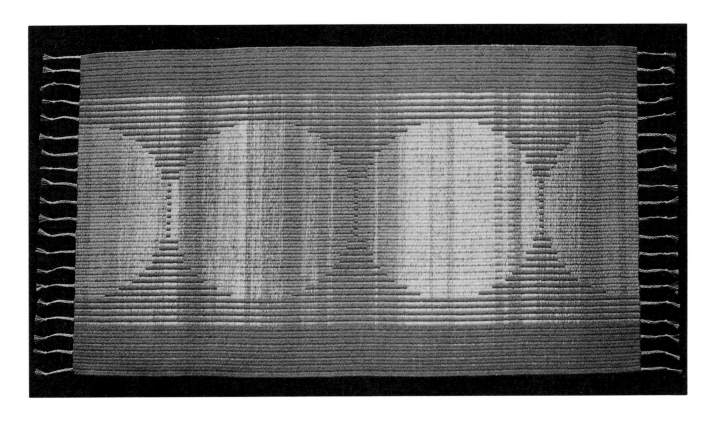

Plate 63 (see p. 128)

Plate 64 (see p. 128)

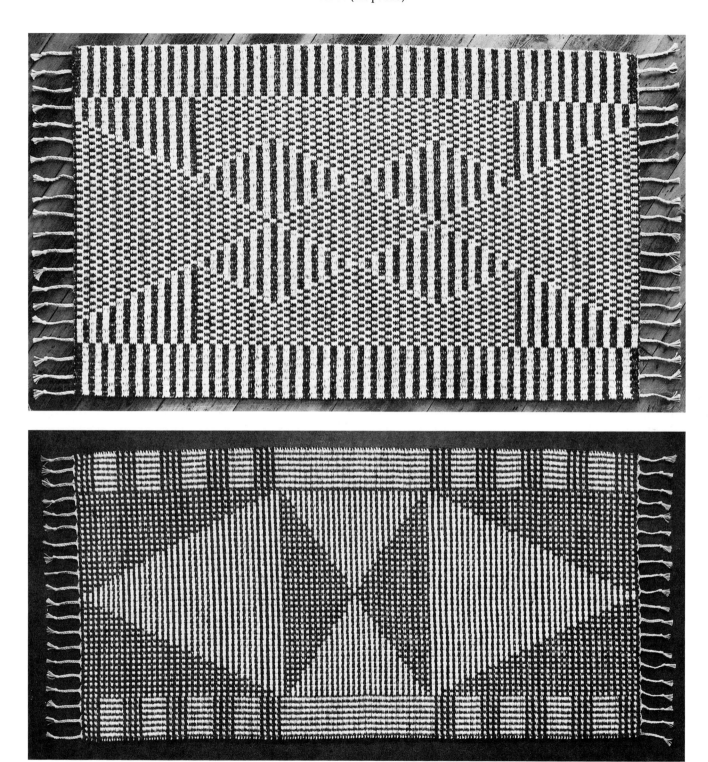

Plate 65 (see p. 128)

Plate 66 (see p. 129)

The warp is sleyed as shown in *Fig. 109(b)*; the pair of pattern ends going together in one dent of an 8 reed. The initial end on shaft 2 at the right, and the final end on shaft 1 at the left should be doubled. A weft of 2-ply carpet wool used two-fold is suitable.

It is possible to apply shaft-switching to this block weave, but for full freedom of design it entails switching a pair of pattern ends from shafts 3 and 4, to 5 and 6, or to 7 and 8. So one end of a pair has to be able to attach to shaft 3 or 5 or 7, and the other to 4 or 6 or 8, as in *Fig. 110(a)*. For convenience of working, it is obviously better to transpose the threading to that in *Fig. 110(b)*, and of course alter the lifts accordingly. Then each end of the pair can be switched between three adjacent shafts; see *Fig. 110(c)*. The set-up for just one of these ends would then be similar to that in *Fig. 101*. But as so many loops would be needed (six for each pair of ends), this is perhaps an instance where a simpler method, like snap hooks, would serve well, at least for an undemanding design.

(b) Three-colour Block Weave Based on the Four-end Draft

As *Fig. 111(a)* shows, this differs from the previous block weave in that there is a pair of pattern ends between every tie-down end on shaft 1 or 2; otherwise it is very similar. The lifts and the shuttle sequence are the same, as is the look of the woven result. The cross-section, *Fig. 111(c)*, shows that the central weft is probably better hidden as it is separated from the front and back weft by more ends.

Fig. 111(a) shows only one repeat of each of the three threading units. Notice the extra end on shaft 2 at the left selvage which is needed to make the three wefts catch satisfactorily. The warp has 9 epi, sleyed in a 6 reed, so a dent with a tie-down end alternates with a dent holding a pair of pattern ends.

Compared with the last block weave, this would require even more preparatory work to set it up for shaft-switching as it has so many pattern ends per inch.

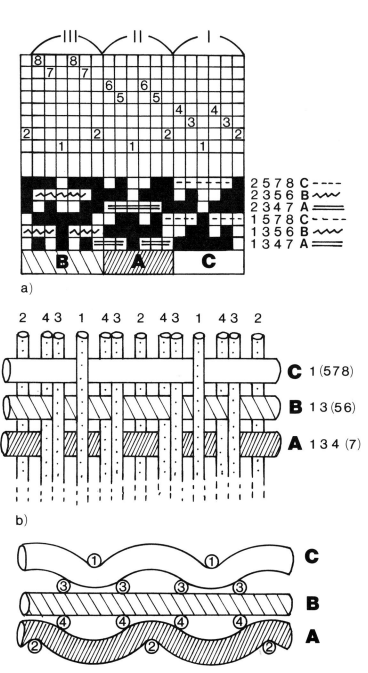

a)

2 5 7 8	C	- - - -
2 3 5 6	B	~~~
2 3 4 7	A	═══
1 5 7 8	C	- - - -
1 3 5 6	B	~~~
1 3 4 7	A	═══

b)

C 1 (578)
B 1 3 (56)
A 1 3 4 (7)

c)

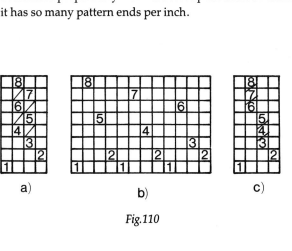

Fig.110

Fig.111

Warp-face Weaves

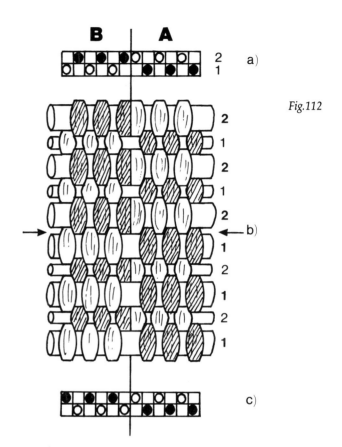

a)

Fig.112

b)

c)

One of the most fruitful fields in warp-face design is the combination of a warp of alternate dark and light ends with a weft of alternate thick and thin yarns.

At its simplest, two shafts, threaded as in *Fig. 112(a)*, can give two blocks. If a thick weft is thrown when shaft 1 is raised and a thin when 2 is raised, then an A block will show mainly dark and a B block mainly light; see *Fig. 112(b)*, lower half. By reversing the thick/thin sequence of the weft (either by throwing the thin twice, or, what is better for strength, the thick twice), the colours of the blocks are counter-changed; see *Fig. 112(b)*, top half above arrows. These are *linked blocks*; when A is dark, B must be light, and vice versa. A cannot change without B also changing.

Note
— *At the junction between blocks A and B, two ends of different colour are both entered on the same shaft. These two ends rise or fall together in every shed; see the junction running down the centre of* Fig. 112(b). *The apparent error could have been avoided by threading two ends of the same colour on different shafts, as in the centre of* Fig. 112(c).

So there are two ways of handling the junction between linked blocks; either keep a constant colour sequence and alter the threading, as at (*a*), or keep a constant threading and alter the colour sequence, as at (*c*). The latter may seem preferable. In more complex multishaft designs, it is unavoidable that, at some junctions between blocks, two adjacent warp ends will move together in this way, no matter which method is used. So it is simpler to make an arbitrary rule that a block always begins on a dark thread and, because it has an even number of threads, always ends on a light one.

Note
— *The width of each block is decided as the warp is threaded (the minimum being two threads); the length of each block in the warp direction is decided during weaving.*

When extending the idea on to four shafts, the four possible blocks can be arranged in several ways; *Fig. 113(a)* shows one of these. It will be seen that blocks A and B are completely

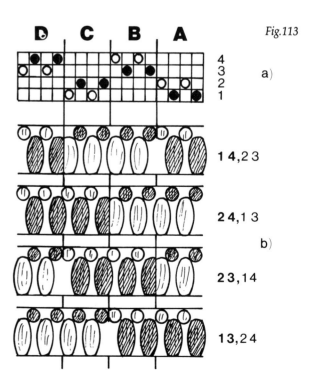

Fig.113

a)

b)

14,23

24,13

23,14

13,24

Plate 67 (see pp. 142,144)

Plate 68 (see pp. 142,144)

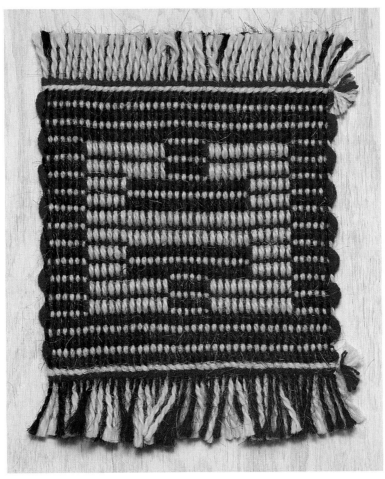

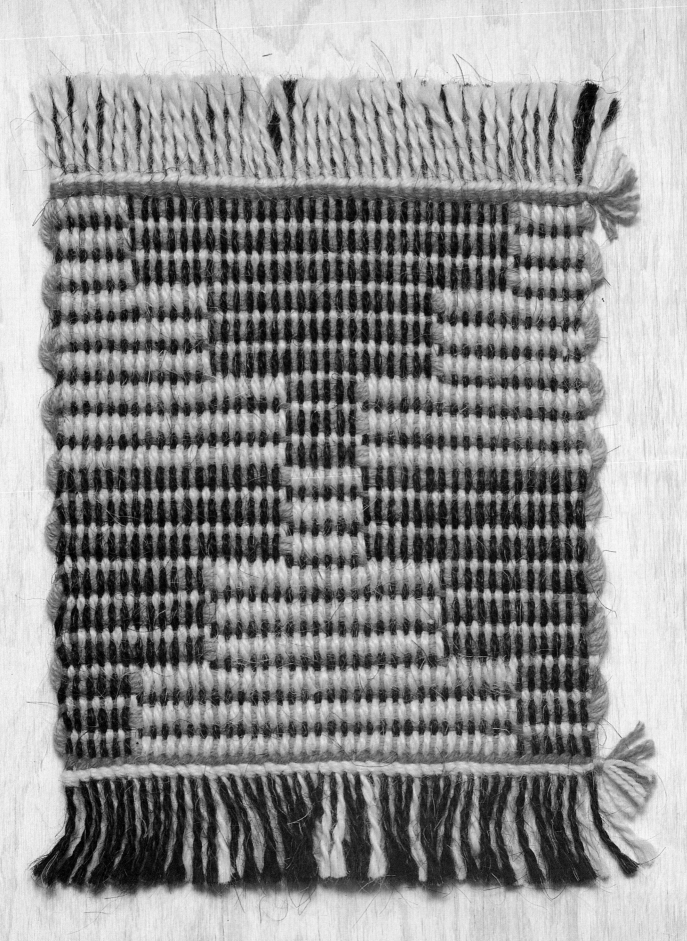

Plate 69 (see pp. 142,144)

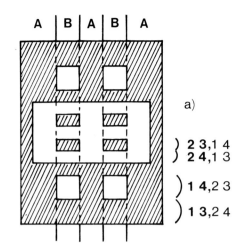

a)

$$\Big\}\ \mathbf{2\ 3,1\ 4}$$
$$\Big\}\ \mathbf{2\ 4,1\ 3}$$

$$\Big\}\ \mathbf{1\ 4,2\ 3}$$

$$\Big\}\ \mathbf{1\ 3,2\ 4}$$

unlinked, so either can appear dark or light, irrespective of how the other appears. Using only these two blocks, designs such as in *Fig. 114(a)* can be produced where the lifts for the thick and thin wefts are shown at the side in heavy and light type respectively.

Note
— *There can be a solid dark border, as in* Fig. 114 (a), *produced by threading part of block A with dark warp on both shafts 1 and 2. Applying this idea to both blocks greatly increases the design possibilities. The narrowest such warpway stripe is naturally two warp ends wide.*

Looking at *Fig. 113(a)* again, it is seen that blocks A and C are linked, i.e. they share the same two shafts but with reversed threading order; similarly, blocks B and D are linked. With this traditional arrangement of the blocks the similarly-coloured threads of any *two adjacent* blocks can be raised together. Thus lifting shafts 1 and 3 brings up the dark ends in blocks A and B, and the light in C and D; lifting shafts 2 and 3 brings the dark ends up in blocks B and C, and so on. This is shown in a very diagrammatic way in *Fig. 113(b)*. As a result, simple designs like that in *Fig. 114(b)* can be woven with the blocks threaded in the sequence shown.

Note
— *Design areas under A and C are similarly arranged but with their colours reversed; hence they can be produced by the linked blocks A and C; the same applies to the areas under B and D.*

Fig. 113(b) shows how, at the first pick of a new design area, the thick weft in some places lies in the same shed as the previous thin weft. This is inevitable, but as it happens in a different place each time, there is no cumulative effect on the fell of the rug.

If, however, the design areas are counter-changed as at the top of *Fig. 114(b)*, the last shed of one area is identical with the first shed of the new area all across the warp. Three possibilities then exist.

1. The last thin weft of the previous area can be omitted, so that two thick wefts follow in succession.
2. The thick and thin wefts can both lie in the same shed; a choice which preserves their side-to-side sequence.
3. The first thick weft of the new area can be omitted so that two thin wefts follow each other; this is not advisable as it weakens the rug.

The threading in *Fig. 113(a)* makes more sense if it is transposed and becomes a member of the well-known shadow weave family. *Fig. 115*, top, shows the previously used threading (with the blocks reduced to their smallest size of two threads each) and, below, the transposition into a shadow weave. At the bottom are the four possible design

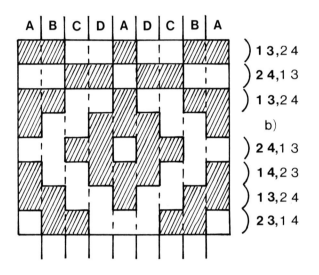

$$\Big\}\ \mathbf{1\ 3,2\ 4}$$
$$\Big\}\ \mathbf{2\ 4,1\ 3}$$
$$\Big\}\ \mathbf{1\ 3,2\ 4}$$

b)

$$\Big\}\ \mathbf{2\ 4,1\ 3}$$
$$\Big\}\ \mathbf{1\ 4,2\ 3}$$
$$\Big\}\ \mathbf{1\ 3,2\ 4}$$
$$\Big\}\ \mathbf{2\ 3,1\ 4}$$

Fig.114

areas with, on the right, the lifts for the shadow weave threading, and on the left those for the other threading. The shadow weave both looks more logical and has the more memorable lifts of a 2/2 twill 'woven on opposites'. It also has the advantage that the ends in a threading block are not on adjacent shafts but are spread out, thus making shedding easier. This is more noticeable with the six- and eight-shaft developments of shadow weave; see *Figs. 116* and *117*.

In all the examples given, the lifts are of course repeated in pairs as often as desired for each design area, the thick and thin wefts alternating. It can be noted here, however, that with only one weft of uniform size and lifting the shafts in (12,23,34,41) order, the shadow weave draft gives a warp-face 2/2 twill 'woven on opposites'.

Fig. 116 shows a six-shaft shadow weave as a point draft and, below, how the block areas will appear if lifted in the conventional sequence, which happens to be the lifts of a 3/3 twill 'woven on opposites'. *Fig. 117* shows a straight draft of an eight-shaft shadow weave, again lifted in the conventional order as a 4/4 twill 'woven on opposites'.

It should be understood when designing that:

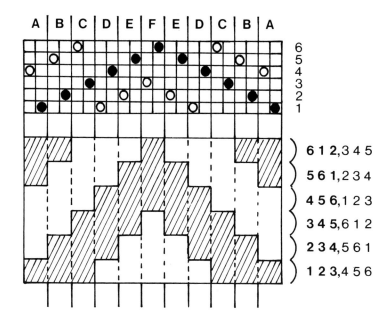

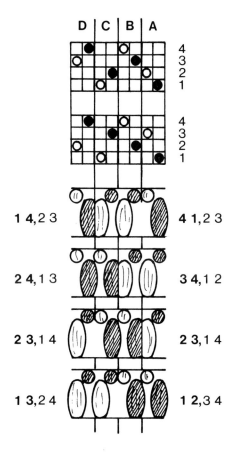

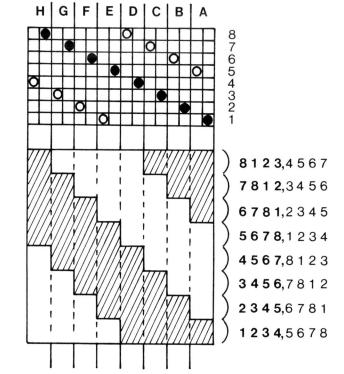

Fig.116

(lifting sequence, Fig.116)
6 1 2,3 4 5
5 6 1,2 3 4
4 5 6,1 2 3
3 4 5,6 1 2
2 3 4,5 6 1
1 2 3,4 5 6

Fig.115

1 4,2 3   4 1,2 3
2 4,1 3   3 4,1 2
2 3,1 4   2 3,1 4
1 3,2 4   1 2,3 4

Fig.117

8 1 2 3,4 5 6 7
7 8 1 2,3 4 5 6
6 7 8 1,2 3 4 5
5 6 7 8,1 2 3 4
4 5 6 7,8 1 2 3
3 4 5 6,7 8 1 2
2 3 4 5,6 7 8 1
1 2 3 4,5 6 7 8

1. The blocks A,B,C and so on do not have to be threaded in that alphabetical order. For example, a (A,D,B,E,C,F) order could be used for the six-shaft version, or any order that produced the desired design.

2. The lifting sequence does not have to follow the order shown, which of course always produces diagonal lines and diamonds.

3. From the point of view of the designing, it may be found easier if the linked blocks are omitted, i.e. if only blocks A to C in the six-shaft version, and A to D in the eight-shaft version are used. This implies that there are three or four completely separate and unrelated areas in the design whose appearance is controlled by the way the shafts are lifted.

The relationship between linked and unlinked blocks can perhaps be demonstrated by considering a simple design like that in the centre of *Fig. 118*. If it is split up into its constituent parts, I to IV, it will be seen that there are four different areas running down the design. Now if this were woven without linked blocks, it would need eight shafts, two for each area; see the draft above and the lifts on the right. But the design shows that areas I and III are identical in design but opposite in colour, and the same applies to areas II and IV. So these areas can be woven on linked blocks and only four shafts are needed; see the bottom of *Fig. 118* and the lifts on the left.

Both drafts produce an identical result. If, however, a solid colour is wanted all across the design, this could easily be obtained with the eight-shaft draft by lifting (1234,5678), but is impossible with the four-shaft draft.

Plates 67, 68 and 69 (pp. 138–9) show samples woven on a pointed variety of the eight-shaft draft in *Fig. 118*.

Practical Details

To produce a true warp-face structure, i.e. one with the weft completely covered, the warp has to be set so close that shedding is difficult. This dictates the type of warp material, which should be as smooth as possible coupled with strength; a hard-twisted worsted or cotton is suitable.

The shedding can be eased by using breaker pedals. If, for instance, shafts 1 and 2 have to be raised for one shed, tie a pedal which raises only 1, and another which raises 2 (or 1

and 2). With one foot press the breaker pedal which raises 1. Make sure this half-shed is clear, then with the other foot add the pedal raising 2 (or 1 and 2). Make sure the full shed is clear and throw the shuttle.

Because of this shedding problem, rugs are often woven which are more warp-dominant than true warp-face. In other words, the weft is visible to a varying degree. If the weft is the same colour as one of the warp materials, areas where it is passing under that warp will appear solid in colour and the other areas striped. The weft can be a colour halfway between the two warp colours and so blend with both; or it can be something quite different. So its partial visibility obviously adds to the design possibilities and means several rugs woven on the same warp can have a slightly different colouring; this was done in the three samples Plates 67–9 (pp. (pp. 138–9), all woven on the same warp of black horsehair and white goathair, set at 8 epi.

The alternation of the thick and thin wefts means they have to be linked at each selvage. One way to improve the selvage is to throw the thin weft in every shed, adding the thick to every other shed. The loop of thick weft at the selvage can be made firmer by twisting it strongly before it is finally positioned and beaten.

It is true that a stronger, harder yarn can be used as the warp in a warp-face rug than as the weft in a weft-face one, suggesting that the former has a more hard-wearing surface. Against this is the fact that it is almost impossible to cram ends in a warp-face rug as closely as wefts are beaten in a weft-face rug. So it is difficult to say which has the better wearing properties.

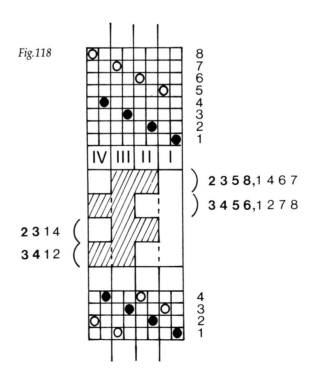

Fig.118

Weft Twining

One or two rows of two-strand weft twining at the start and end of a rug make a strong, firm, intermediate line between the woven structure of the rug itself and whatever finish is employed. The yarn used can be the same as the warp (perhaps three- or four-fold) in which case the twining blends in visually with the rug finish; or it can be some coloured yarn, such as the rug weft (again using several thicknesses), in which case the twining becomes decorative as well as practical.

There is a simple way of working two rows of twining simultaneously and, if two colours are used, these rows can produce six different small-scale patterns; see *Fig. 119(a)* to *(f)*. These result from the three possible ways of arranging the colours at the start, as in *Fig. 119(i)* to *(iii)*; and on working either in countered twining, i.e. a row of S- above a row of Z-twining or vice versa, as in *Fig. 119(a), (c)* and *(e)*; or working both rows in S- or both in Z-twining, as in *Fig. 119(b), (d)* and *(f)*.

The top six rows in Plate 70 (pp. 146–7) correspond exactly with rows *(a)* to *(f)* in *Fig. 119*.

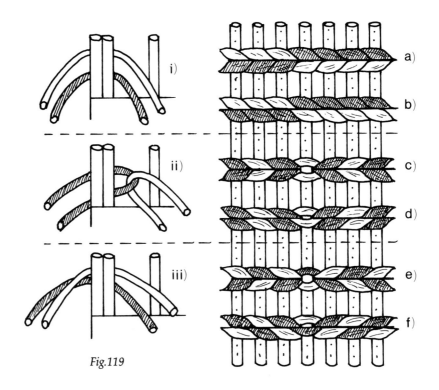

Fig.119

Countered Twining

This is by far the easier of the two types and with practice takes no longer to work than a single row of twining.

Start with two long strands centred under the selvage end; *Fig. 120(a)*.

Open the right-hand pair, A and B, and pass the left-hand pair, C and D, to the right between them; see (*b*).

Immediately pass C and D under the next warp end; see (*c*).

Again open the right-hand pair, (which is now C and D), and pass the left-hand pair, A and B, between them and under the next warp end; see (*d*).

Continuing thus gives a row of Z-twining above a row of S-twining.

If the strands being used are of two colours and are arranged as in *Fig. 119(i)*, a white row will lie above a black; see *Fig. 119(a)*, left, and Plate 70 (pp. 146–7) top row and both ends of warp-face samples in Plates 67–9 (pp. 138–9).

If the strands are arranged as in *Fig. 119(ii)*, linked into each other, the two rows appear as alternating chevrons of the two colours; see *Fig. 119(c)*, left, and Plate 70 third row down.

If they are arranged as in *Fig. 119(iii)*, the pattern, seen at (*e*) and Plate 70 (pp. 146–7) fifth row down, is produced.

Variations

1. To reverse the twining direction as at the centres of *Fig. 119 (c)* and (*e*), pass the right-hand pair through the left-hand pair which then goes under the next warp end; i.e. the exact opposite of the previously described movement. See centre of third and fifth row down in Plate 70 (pp. 146–7).

2. In pattern (*a*), the colours are easily counter-changed as shown at the centre. When two strands have been passed under a warp end, as in *Fig. 120(c)*, cross them so D is now above C. Now open C and D and pass A and B through between them. Pass A and B behind the next warp end and again cross these so B is above A. Once these two crossings have been made, the work proceeds normally with the coloured lines reversed. This has happened twice in top row of Plate 70 (pp. 146–7).

3. If only the first of the above crossings is made and the twining continued normally, then pattern *Fig. 119(e)* is produced. See right-hand end of bottom row in Plate 70 (pp. 146–7).

4. To move from pattern (*a*) to (*c*). See *Fig. 121*, top. After C and D have been passed through between A and B, bring down C (the upper black) and pass it under the next warp end, 3. Bring D up, double twist it with A (the other black strand) which itself then goes behind warp end 3.

5. To move from pattern (*c*) to (*a*); see *Fig. 121*, bottom. Pass C and D through the opened A and B. Bring the

upper black, C, down and pass it under warp end 3. Give a double twist to the lower white and black, B and D; bring B upwards and place it behind end 3.

Though a little difficult to master, the above two transitions have a neat appearance, and can be seen on bottom row in Plate 70 (pp. 146–7).

Two Rows of S- or of Z-twining

Start as for countered twining, but when the right-hand pair, A and B, are opened pass only the lower of the left-hand pair through, i.e. D, and pass the upper of the pair, C, over them. So the four strands interpenetrate as shown in *Fig. 120(e)*. Continuing thus gives two rows of S-twining.

To make two rows of Z-twining, pass the upper of the left-hand pair, i.e. C, through between A and B; and pass the lower, D, under them, giving the situation shown in *Fig. 120(f)*.

Of the three possible patterns in two colours shown in *Fig. 119(b)*, (*d*) and (*f*), the latter is perhaps the most striking with its strong oblique stripes; see sixth row down in Plate 70 (pp. 146–7).

Alternating the above S- and Z-twining manoeuvres gives four picks of plain weave. So starting with the colours arranged as in *Fig. 119(ii)*, woven pick-and-pick stripes are produced.

Using the above manipulations, it is possible to move from any one pattern to another, mid-row; such transitions can be related to the design of the rug itself.

When the right selvage is reached, tie the four strands in a temporary knot. Later these can be braided when the rug is being finished. If a braid is wanted at all four corners of the rug, start the twining by knotting the four strands together, leaving enough length to be braided later.

Each of the four strands should be 20–40 inches (50–100 cm) longer than the width of the rug, depending on the length of braids wanted. They should be of such thickness that when they are pulled tight after each movement, the warp sett is unaltered. This is usually a little thicker than the weft yarn being used for the woven structure.

Taaniko Twining

If immediately after the left-hand pair have been passed through the right-hand pair the movement is repeated (with the *new* left-hand pair going through the *new* right-hand pair), a double twist will be given to the twining pairs exactly as in Taaniko twining. This enormously enlarges the design possibilities as a colour can be kept on the surface as long as desired and then changed by making only a single twist, as at the centre of *Fig. 122*. Its use is limited, however, because it is a one-sided technique.

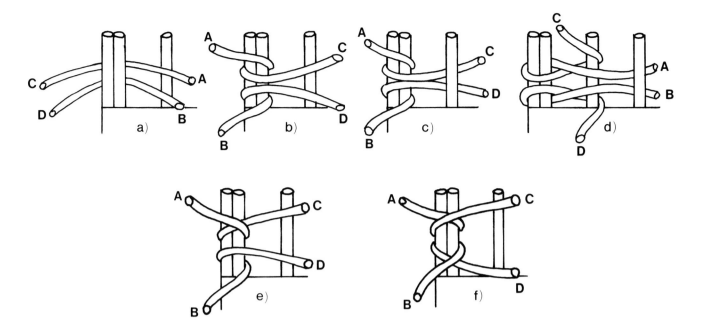

Fig.120

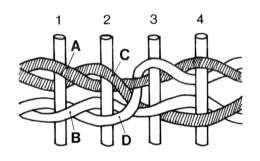

Fig.121

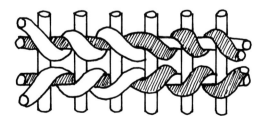

Fig.122

Plate 70 (see p. 144)

Rug Finishes

Weft Protector

This finish was seen being worked on a weft-face camel-hair rug in Rajasthan, India. The rug had been made on a horizontal ground loom so its warp ends were loops which had been lapped around the end bars of the loom. These uncut loops were the elements used in the finish, but for simplicity single ends are here described and illustrated.

Starting at the right edge, take the second end down to the left across ends 3 and 4, then up to the right behind them, emerging between ends 2 and 3, pointing upwards; see *Fig. 123(a)*. This is a common knot or hitch used in many weft protectors. Before it is tightened, take the first end over end 2 and down between ends 3 and 4, as in *Fig. 123(b)*. Discard end 3.

Knot end 4 around ends 1 and 5 with the same knot as used before; the result is shown in *Fig. 123(c)*. Again, before this is tightened, take end 2 over end 4 and down between ends 1 and 5, as indicated by the dotted line and arrow. Discard end 1.

Knot 5 around 2 and 6; take 4 over 5 and down between 2 and 6. Discard end 2.

This sequence is repeated. Always knot a single end around two ends (one of which is the next unused end to the left, the other is the one brought down from the right), then bring the end which lies to the right, pointing upwards, over the single end and down between the two ends. Discard the right-hand of the two ends.

Adjust the tension after every repeat, pulling one of the relevant ends upwards, the other downwards. The result on the upper surface looks like two rows of countered twining; see *Fig. 123(d)*, where the part contributed by one end is shaded. The edge is secure as, once it is established, each end is involved in two knots. It was worked across twice in the Indian example seen.

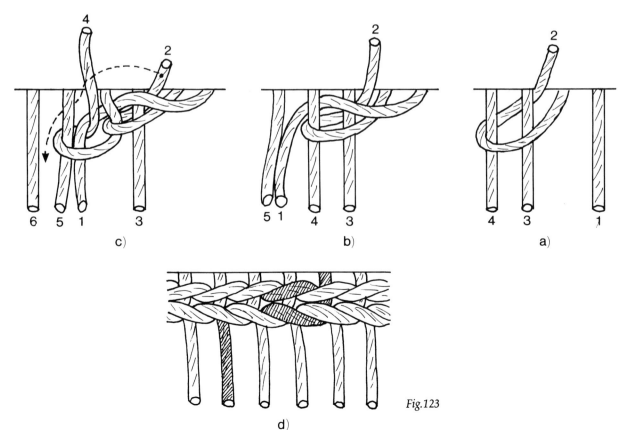

Fig.123

Preparing the End of the Rug for Large Braids

If a few large braids, rather than many small ones, are wanted at the end of a rug, a neatly structured way has to be found of gathering the warp ends together for each braid; otherwise the outermost threads of a group lie loose and unprotected. A traditional method, seen on some Middle Eastern rugs, builds up a triangle in which the warp ends wrap around each other, working towards the centre of the group, from which the braid then springs. It is done as follows.

There should be an odd number of ends in each group; only eleven are used here in the description and diagrams, but more would probably be used in reality. So end 6 is the central one.

Start at the right side of the rug and imagine the ends numbered 1 to 11 from right to left, as in *Fig. 124(a)*.

Wrap end 1 round 2,3,4,5 and 6. Bring it down to lie beside 6, so there are now two ends in the centre; see *Fig. 124(a)*. The wrapping movement is the one sometimes called locking soumak.

Now wrap 11 around 10,9,8,7 and finally around the two central ends, 6 and 1. Bring 11 down to lie beside 6 and 1, to make three central ends; see *Fig. 124(b)*.

Wrap 2 around 3,4,5 and the central three, then bring it down to make four in the centre; see *Fig. 124(c)*.

Wrap 10 around 9,8,7 and the central four, and so on.

Continue in this way, always wrapping the outermost thread from right, then left, into the centre. As this central group grows, the nearby ends are forced outwards.

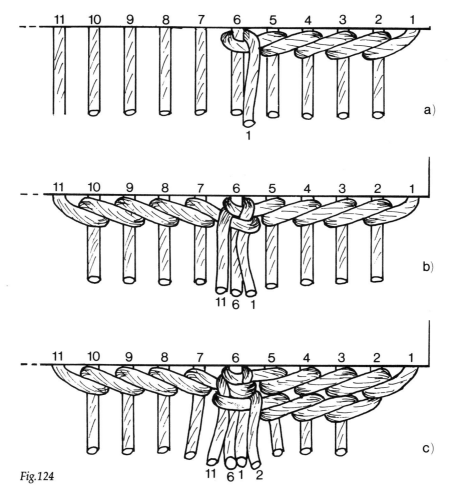

Fig.124

Plate 71 (see p. 152)

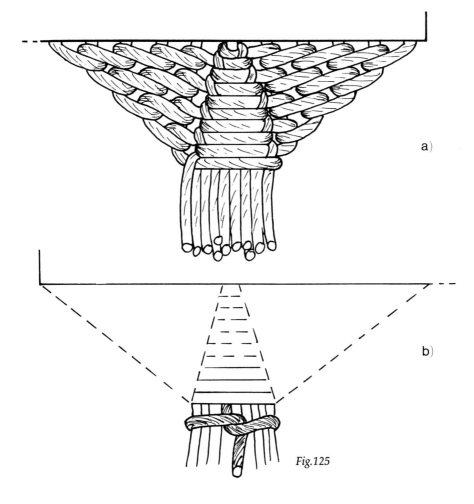

a)

b)

Fig.125

The two final wraps will be of end 5 around the central nine ends, then end 7 around the central ten. The triangle of wrapping will then look as in *Fig. 125(a)* and Plate 71 (pp. 150–1).

Now, at the *back*, select one end and tie it in a hitch, as shown in *Fig. 125(b)*, to hold everything secure before the braiding begins.

The odd number of elements is a slight disadvantage if the braid is to be a square braid, which needs an even number to give a perfectly symmetrical structure. For instance, if a four-strand is now to be worked, one of the strands will consist of only two ends, compared with the other three strands of three ends each (making the total of eleven). But this slight imbalance is hardly noticeable in the finished braid. Starting with an even number of ends (preferably divisible by four), would give a perfect braid but it would come out of the wrapped triangle a little off-centre.

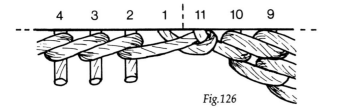

Fig.126

Working the next group of eleven ends to the left, start with end 1 as before. But first take it round end 11 of the previous group, as shown in *Fig. 126*, then wrap it round 2,3 and so on, as before. This is done to avoid any gap between adjacent groups where weft could bulge outwards.

The back of this structure has a different, but still neat, appearance.

Whipping

The normal way of whipping the end of a braid on a rug finish uses an extra length of yarn. In a very neat method, employed by the camel-girth-makers in Rajasthan, one of the elements of the braid itself is tied into a constrictor knot of the type shown, in an untightened state, in *Fig. 127*. It is made as follows; see *Fig. 128(a)* to *(e)*.

1. Tie a knot at the lower end of the element to be used so it can be recognized in later stages. Then pull a long loop forwards and twist it clockwise, securing the crossing point with the left thumb; spot in (*a*).
2. As shown by the arrow, carry the loop behind the braid with the right hand; see (*b*).

3. Bring its lower part over the threads in front and take a new grip with the left thumb to hold it in place; spot in (c). Let the loop fall downwards behind the braid. Slip the whole of the braid backwards through the loop; arrow in (c). Push the loop upwards, as in (d).

4. Pull the first wrap really tight.

5. Repeat stages 2 and 3 with the new loop, i.e. take it behind as shown by the arrow and so on. Do this three or four times, making sure that each wrap lies above the previous one (i.e. nearer the rug), and that it is as tight as possible. It will then look as in (e).

6. Finally pull down on the knotted end of the wrapping element to tighten; arrow in (e).

If at any stage, the loop becomes too small to manipulate, draw up some slack from the knotted end.

The knot can of course be worked with a separate element, perhaps a different colour or material from the warp. In this case, the wraps need not be made so tightly, because both ends of the element can be pulled in the final stage, one upwards, one downwards, thus taking up any slack in the wraps.

Fig.127

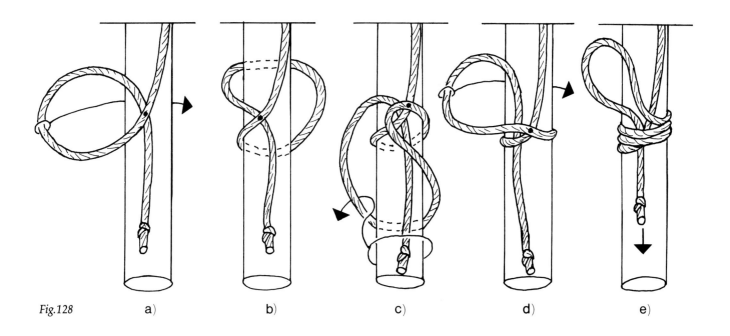

Fig.128 a) b) c) d) e)

General Workshop Notes

Loom and Workshop Equipment

Bench height

Weave with the bench or loom seat as high as possible. This is because the more the arms incline downwards, rather than forwards, to the batten and shuttles, the less strain is put on the shoulder and neck muscles. Also, the more nearly straight the leg is when depressing a pedal, the stronger the force it can exert.

Loom light

A fluorescent light as long as the loom is wide will give good shadowless illumination. Hang it directly over the average position of the fell of the rug and use a colour-matching tube.

Shuttle catcher

If the cloth-protecting strip of wood, often positioned in front of the breast beam (TRW p. 54), is raised ¾ inch (19 mm), it will stop shuttles from falling off when beating.

Weighting the batten

A more heavily weighted batten than previously advised – e.g. 1 lb per inch (180 gm per cm) of batten width – may seem cumbersome at first, but very soon feels normal. Combined with a straight-armed backward pull it gives a really efficient beat; only one such beat is necessary after each pick.

Marking the centre of the batten in some way, e.g. with a dome-headed nail, acts as a visible and palpable guide which ensures the two hands are equidistant from the centre when beating.

Universal tie-ups for countermarch looms

Fig. 129 shows two different universal pedal-to-lam tie-ups for a four-shaft countermarch loom; A being devised by the late Lore Yongmark, B by myself. Once made they never have to be changed, because by depressing *two* pedals at a time, one with each foot, all the fourteen sheds possible with four shafts can be obtained.

Of the eight pedals in use (A to H), the four on the left (worked by the left foot) control only two shafts – 1 and 3 in Method A, 1 and 2 in Method B – being unattached to the other two shafts which are controlled by the four pedals on the right (worked by the right foot).

The sheds are produced as follows.

	Lifts	Method A	Method B
Plain Weave	13	B + H	C + E
	24	A + G	D + F
2/2 Twill	12	D + E	B + H
	23	C + E	D + E
	34	C + F	A + G
	41	D + F	C + F
1/3 Twill	1	D + H	C + H
	2	A + E	D + H
	3	C + H	A + E
	4	A + F	A + F
3/1 Twill	123	B + E	B + E
	234	C + G	D + G
	341	B + F	C + G
	412	D + G	B + F

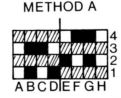

METHOD A

A B C D E F G H

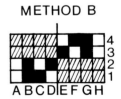

METHOD B

A B C D E F G H

■ = Tie to lower or longer lam, so shaft rises

☐ = Tie to upper or shorter lam, so shaft falls

▨ = Do not tie to either lam

Fig.129

Gate for pedals

A wooden frame with uprights separating the pedals, known as a gate, can prove helpful. It is fixed under the loom in front of the pedal-to-lam ties; see *Fig. 130*. It prevents any side-to-side swinging of the pedals which are therefore always exactly where the feet expect them to be. The gate can also be used to make the pedals fan out as they pass from the back to the front of the loom; see Plate 72 (p. 156).

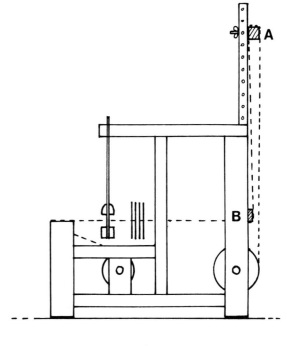

Fig.131

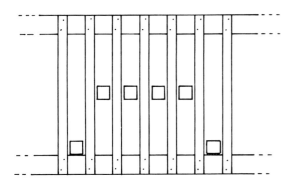

Fig.130

Warp extender

The extension advised for difficult warps (TRW p. 54) combined with a sectional warp beam, really solves all problems of even warp tension for the rug weaver. As previously described, this extends horizontally backwards and takes up much space; but the idea works equally well if the extension is upwards; see *Fig. 131* and left-hand loom in Plate 72 (p. 156).

The extension pieces can be slotted angle iron fixed to the inside of the back uprights of the loom as shown. To these the cross-bar, A, is bolted. The warp passes from the warp beam up to and over A, then down and under B to the shafts. A, which may initially have to be reached by ladder, is gradually lowered as more warp is wanted, the beam never being touched during the weaving of a rug.

A rug loom with a more sophisticated control of A is seen in Plate 72 (centre). A small handle at one side turns two threaded rods in unison and these, passing through A, control its height with ease and accuracy.

A raddle, fixed on top of A or near it, should be used to keep threads parallel in their long journey from beam to shafts. The raddle should have at least 3 or 4 dents per inch.

When a rug has been woven, wind on the cloth beam until the last picks of the rug are some way under the breast beam. Now release the warp beam and move the bar A to its furthest or highest position, drawing warp from the beam for the next rug; then fix the beam again. Only now cut the rug from the loom, leaving at least 10 inches (25 cm) of warp for the fringe. This sequence of first moving the cross bar then cutting the rug off avoids several problems.

Beaming the warp

Using the above warp extender, the only requirement in beaming the warp is that the ends go on so tightly that they do not shift during weaving. A warped beam with an uneven surface, which would normally lead to progressively worse tension problems, is acceptable because the length of warp going into the rug is *off* the beam before weaving starts and so stays at a perfectly even tension. This implies that, when using a sectional beam, a tensioner less elaborate than the one formerly described (TRW p. 64) is adequate. For instance, the common tensioner with a set of dowels works well as long as the drag on the warp is increased by wrapping ends round one or more dowels, as shown in *Fig. 132*.

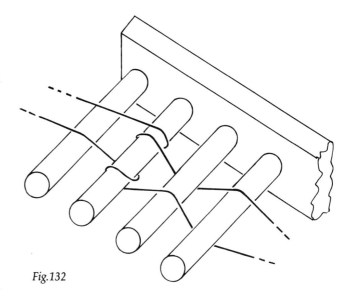

Fig.132

Plate 72 (above): Warp extender on the rug loom designed by the author and Harrisville Designs (Harrisville, NH, 03450, USA).

Storing ski shuttles

Ski shuttles can be neatly and compactly stored hung on wooden dowels. Find the maximum size of dowel which will fit under the hooked end and fix it horizontally into the wall. Shuttles can then be threaded on to the dowel, facing alternately to right and to left, to take up least space; see *Fig. 133*.

Bumping bar or donkey

To make sure a skein unwinds easily and without tangling, it should first be 'bumped'. Slip it over the end of a strong, smooth bar (the bumping bar or donkey) – e.g. a length of old warp beam bolted to the loom frame. Take care that the correct opening of the skein is made; see *Fig. 134*. Then insert two hands into the lower loop from opposite sides and bang downwards (see arrow), slip the skein round a little, bump it again and so on. Doing this will make previously loose threads disappear and the skein will gradually return to the ordered state it was in when first made. Transfer it carefully to the skeiner and it should unwind with no trouble.

Tying hanks

If tying hanks for dyeing or washing, make a minimum of three equidistant ties, one where the two ends of the threads are joined, and two other figure-of-eight ties using a contrasting material or colour. Then if the skein is held up by one tie there is always another at the side which can be pulled outwards to find the opening of the skein, as in *Fig. 134*.

Skeiner

Carpet wool sometimes comes in very large skeins which will just slide off a skeiner of the umbrella type, especially if it is set up with the axle vertical. It is best to have a skeiner which revolves round a horizontal axis. Then it can be used for winding skeins (by inserting a stick into the spokes to make a turning handle) as well as for unwinding them. Here, as anywhere in the workshop, industrial equipment if obtainable will probably outlast any equipment made specifically for handworkers.

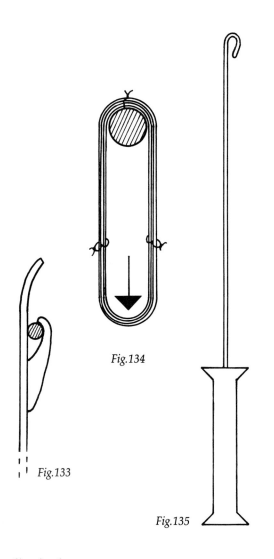

Fig.134

Fig.133

Fig.135

Threading hooks

Most hooks have an end with a stamped-out notch. Though well suited to normal warps they are troublesome with a thick rug warp, especially if two or more ends are drawn in together through one heddle eye. Much more satisfactory is a hook made of stiff wire, mounted in a handle, such as a wooden bobbin; see *Fig. 135*. The wire should be about ¹⁄₂₀ inch (1.25 mm) in diameter and the whole can be about 8 to 10 inches (20 – 25 cm) long. Such a hook will handle several ends at once and, being smooth, cannot snag or split the warp material.

Temples

Very neat temples are now available from Finland. Being made of metal, they are strong without being bulky and without obscuring the part just woven. They allow ²⁄₅ inch (1cm) adjustments in length, which, though not ideal, is adequate. When the temple is inserted right at the start of the rug, be sure that some pins are not imbedded in the front stick, if wooden, and then snapped off by the beating.

Weaving

Tying linen

Linen rug warp has strength but also an annoying slipperiness. But, remember, this vanishes if the linen is damp. For example, when tying to the front stick, a licked finger applied to the relevant part of the yarn will ensure that the first half of a square (reef) knot will not slip while the second is tied.

Also, when working a weft protector, like the Damascus Edge, keep dabbing water (with small paint brush) on to the next few ends where they emerge from the rug and the simple knots will not shift.

Opening warp groups

Weaving the heading picks under tension increases their ability to spread the warp. Pull each pick tight, then catch it around the end of the front stick (to prevent pull-in) before throwing it back. If the fell, so produced, has a slight curve, straighten it with some extra picks just at the edge, as in *Fig. 136*.

Weft yarn

The carpet wool often referred to in the text has a count of about 2/50 . This means it is 2-ply and has 50 yards to the ounce; i.e. 800 yards to the pound, (1600 metres to the kg).

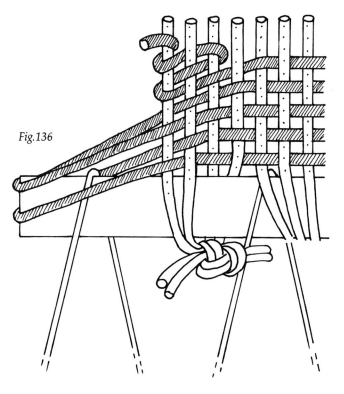

Fig.136

Of course, other yarns of other counts can be used; the ideal wool yarn being 2- or 3-ply, worsted-spun from long staple wool and with a fairly light twist. A highly twisted yarn will not cover the warp so easily. Remember that the *visible* thickness of a possible weft yarn is of little relevance because it is the size it will compress to when woven and beaten in which is important. So overtwist it and roll between the fingers to get an impression of its compressed size and then compare this with the recommended carpet wool, similarly twisted and tested.

A rough and generous estimate for the weft of a flat-weave rug is ½lb per square foot or 2.5kg per square metre.

It is always useful to know which yarns in a workshop can be snapped by hand and which need to be cut with scissors. I know I can break three strands of 2-ply carpet wool (the thickness I often use on a shuttle), but not four strands. Searching for scissors to cut easily breakable threads wastes time.

Weft tension

Always remember to pull slightly on the weft coming from the selvage before throwing the shuttle into the next shed, in order to eliminate the small degree of slack which inevitably exists in the last few inches of the previous pick. Failure to do this leads to vertical ridges of loose weft near both selvages.

Using a ski shuttle

Wind the weft round the two hooks in a circular, not figure of eight, manner, as the latter increases the depth of the loaded shuttle thus making throwing harder.

Without even looking, the weaver should be able to catch a ski shuttle somewhere near its centre as it emerges from the shed. The eyes should be fixed on the selvage the shuttle has just left, ensuring the weft is properly positioned and tensioned there. Practice this with an empty shuttle.

Only unwind from the shuttle enough weft for the next pick. Working with a great length of slack weft which has to be hauled through every shed is very time-consuming.

A ski shuttle, unless overloaded with weft, should pass easily through a shed only 2 inches (5 cm) deep. So the large, much-favoured, sheds produced with a jack loom on a lightly tensioned warp are not necessary; in fact, with a correctly taut linen warp they are impossible to make. I ask weavers with this deep shed obsession whether they intend to crawl through themselves, dragging the weft behind them.

There is a tendency for the hook on a ski shuttle to catch a warp thread as it enters the small half-shed above a floating selvage. This can be avoided if the shuttle is slightly twisted at this moment, so that the hook is more towards the reed and its underside more towards the weaver. Once past this danger point, it is straightened and thrown normally.

Beating

In rug weaving, beating does not require finesse as the weaver is usually beating as hard as possible. It is not like the controlled or varied beat required in fine weaving. Only when weaving a narrow sample does the heavy beat have to be modified otherwise an over thick fabric will be woven, which is impossible to reproduce at full width. An overslung batten can act as a pendulum giving a regular speed to the weaving. After a weft is beaten, the batten swings back freely, then forwards, then back again. By this time, the next shuttle should be poised and ready for throwing and, while the non-throwing hand holds the batten in that backward position, it is shot across and the cycle repeated.

Darning in weft

A suitable wire to use when darning in the weft ends with a needle and wire loop is an unwound guitar string with a diameter of .016 or .017 inch. One of these will make four or five loops. Simply double over an 8-inch length. Make a handle by bending over the cut ends, as shown in *Fig. 137*, wrapping tightly with yarn to bury the sharp points and then dipping in glue. Alternatively, the wire can be fixed into a proper handle; an Exacto knife handle works well.

An even simpler darning-in implement is made by tying a loop of fine strong yarn through the eye of the darning needle, making the knot as small as possible. The weft end is placed through this loop and as the needle is darned down into the rug in the usual way it draws the weft in after it. So the weft is never actually threaded through the needle's eye.

A magnet fitted to some upright of the loom near the breast beam is a simple and efficient way of holding the needle and threader.

Fig.137

Floating selvages

All selvage problems can be solved in rug weaving by using a floating selvage – i.e. by leaving the outermost working end on each side unthreaded through the shafts, but sleyed normally through the reed. The shuttle always enters a shed by passing over the floating selvage and always leaves by passing under the floating selvage at the opposite side. The latter will happen naturally if the height of this selvage is carefully adjusted.

But this rule, if followed blindly, can lead to over-long weft floats at either selvage. So if a floating selvage is in use, the weft both when entering and leaving the shed must negotiate the floating selvage in a way which avoids such a float. It may take several repeats of a pattern sequence to arrive at the neatest solution, but once found it should be adhered to.

Unweaving

Preserving the weft

Sometimes, when using a complex weave or a pick-up technique, it is hard to trace in reverse sequence the sheds which were used and so release the weft. One solution is to use the weft itself as a leash.

On a flat warp, pull up a loop of weft from the last pick, as shown in *Fig. 138(a)* (which does not show a complex weave). This will lift ends 1,3 and 5 and so allow the shuttle to pass under them to the left and draw out this section of weft.

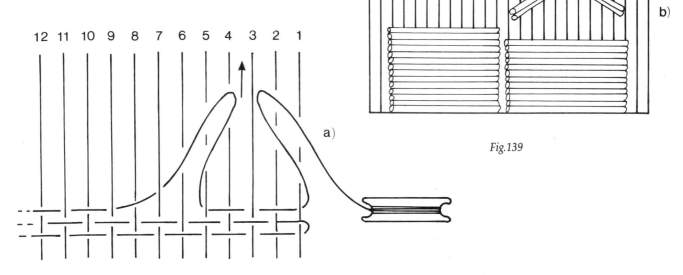

Fig.139

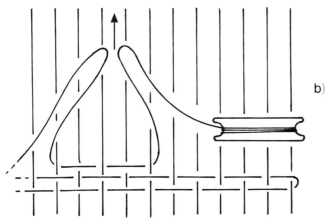

Fig.138

Now pull up another loop to the left, as in *Fig. 138(b)*. Working like this all across the warp, first to the left and then to the right, each pick can be extracted slowly but surely.

Destroying the weft

Occasionally, pressure of time or a cheap weft make the following method preferable.

Cut through the weft in three places, carefully inserting the scissor blade *between* two warp ends. As the dotted lines in the diagrammatic *Fig. 139(a)* show, cut at the centre and close to each selvage. The small outer sections can be easily pulled out by hand. To remove a central section, repeatedly drag a large needle up over its top edge. This will push up several lengths of weft which the other hand can remove; see *Fig. 139(b)*.

Conclusion

Remember that, in all the operations of handweaving, it is regularity which is the aim. Visible irregularities which say 'This is handwoven' usually say, as well, 'This is badly handwoven'. Luckily the loom is a fairly advanced bit of machinery and it only requires the hands and feet to do relatively simple and unskilled actions. There is nothing in weaving requiring the manual skill possessed by a potter. A beginning weaver can press a pedal as 'skilfully' as an experienced professional. The one skill vital to the weaver is the ability to judge tension in threads. As there is no operation in ordinary life requiring this sensitivity, it has to be gradually acquired until an evenly tight warp can be tied to the front stick and an evenly relaxed weft laid in the shed. To spend time tying and retying a warp only to have the teacher point out loose groups is one of the humiliations suffered by every learning weaver. Good equipment helps, but sensitivity to thread tension has to exist in the weaver's hands before a good rug can be woven.